THE HONOR OF KINGS

Proverbs 25:2 It is the glory of God to conceal a thing:
but the honor of kings is to search out a matter.

THE HONOR OF KINGS

Proverbs 25:2 It is the glory of God to conceal a thing: but the honor of kings is to search out a matter.

DAVID RAVELLA

THE HONOR OF KINGS by David Ravella

ISBN: 978-1-59755-727-6

Published by: ADVANTAGE BOOKS™ Longwood, Florida, USA
www.advbookstore.com

Library of Congress Catalog Number: 2023935241

Name: Ravella, David, Author
Title: ***The Honor Of Kings***
David Ravella
Advantage Books 2023
Identifiers: ISBN: 9781597557276, eBook: 9781597557382
Subjects Christian Life: Inspirational
Biblical Studies: Old Testament

Cover Design by Shane Thornton

First Printing: May 2023
23 24 25 26 27 28 10 9 8 7 6 5 4 3 2 1

Table of Contents

Preface

As I woke from sleep one Sunday morning, I suddenly saw Jesus standing before me. His arm was outstretched with keys in His hand. He then said to me, *"This is when David ate the shewbread in the temple."*

Not a moment before the vision ended, I knew that Jesus was in hell after His crucifixion. I was also given the correlation between David and his men being kept from women for three days and Jesus being kept from His church, the *"women,"* for three days as well. In an instant, I was revealed the centerpiece of one of the clearest gospel stories hidden within the Old Testament.

Enthralled, I grabbed my Bible and hasted into my prayer closet. I found the account where David met Ahimelech, the priest, and began to read. Now, I certainly started to read… but Jesus took over! I sat in wonder like a child would when hearing a new bedtime story read to them by their father.

This vision itself was based on 1st Samuel 21. When the chapter was through, I felt impressed to flip to the one right before it. Sure enough, 1st Samuel 20 connected perfectly. In fact, the twentieth chapter so clearly depicts Jesus that I could hardly refrain myself! For lack of better words, I was blown away.

After finishing these two chapters, the thought came to me, *"If chapter twenty-two depicts the resurrection of Jesus... I don't know how I'll be able to handle it!"* Well, as you may have guessed, it certainly did. After Jesus finished reading to me, all I could do was lift my hands and bless the Living God.

After this remarkable encounter, I was left with a treasure of immeasurable worth. I was revealed by the Lord how 1st Samuel chapters 20, 21, and 22 depict the death, burial, and resurrection of Jesus Christ.

If *The Honor Of Kings* could be summed up in an experience rather than a statement, it would have to be the vision and the revelation I received. Though the vision was revealed to me personally, it is by no means private.

What Jesus revealed is for all of us to come to know and understand. He is the hidden treasure buried within the pages of His Word.

Though I was reading about David, Jonathan, and Saul, I realized it's not about them at all… *it's all about Jesus*. He is the whole point of our pursuit! He is the matter worth searching for! My friends, this is the honor of kings.

> *"It is the glory of God to conceal a thing: but the honour of kings is to search out a matter." (Proverbs 25:2)*

Introduction

The purpose of reading God's Word is not to memorize scripture or to study the Old or New Testament accounts alone but to know why they are written in the first place. Although it is evident to see what Jesus did within the Gospels, seeing Him prior to His incarnation is not always as clear. Some aspects of the Old Testament seem to portray God in a different light than Jesus walked in while on the earth. Some may read the Old Covenant and think, *"Did Jesus come to merely appease the Father's wrath?* To answer plainly, *certainly not!* Jesus came to reveal His steadfast love!

Concerning God's "change" of nature, most of us know this is easily refuted when understanding sin and its devastating repercussions. God didn't change… we did! Our nature was changed, which convoluted our perspective of His. Sadly, some of us who have been forgiven still fail to see God for who He truly is. Like a curtain blocks the sunlight, so are the many eyes of those who presently love God still covered today. With that said, I believe that nearly all the fault is found to be with the devil.

The devil relentlessly seeks to keep our eyes closed to God's goodness. He doesn't ever want us to wholly trust God. Even when open, he still manages to distort our view! He shrouds layer upon layer of lies and convinces us that God is somehow holding something back from us. This was the same tactic he used against Eve. The devil instigated mankind's fall by convincing them that God wasn't good. He came in between man's relationship with the Lord and seeks to do the same with us today.

The blood of the Lamb has redeemed us, yet the devil is still the culprit of nearly all our misconceptions of God. The Lord knows that if we were only to see Him through curtainless glass, all our doubts would be dispelled. Therefore, *The Honor of Kings* aims to remove the curtains altogether. The devil has used circumstances, experiences, and misunderstood scriptures to cloud our view of the Lord. He is the thief that has blinded our eyes to our wonderful, unchanging God all along.

Furthermore, the Bible says that it is the glory of God to conceal a thing, but it is the honor of kings to search out a matter (Proverbs 25:2). We have somehow lost sight of what we have been searching for because we have been deceived in thinking we've already attained it. Paul explains this quite well:

> *"Not as though I had already attained, either were already perfect:* ***but I follow after, if that I may apprehend*** *that for which also I am apprehended of Christ Jesus." (Philippians 3:12) (emphasis mine)*

Though we have been apprehended and captured by the love of God, we now have the opportunity to reciprocate. Like a game of tag, it is now our turn to chase Him. We now have this high honor of seeking after Him, and we mustn't let anything get in our way! The way we search for Him today is by reading the Bible with the intention of finding Jesus. Whether that be in the book of Job, Jeremiah, Numbers, or Judges, Jesus is the glory of God concealed.

Being that it is the honor of kings to search out the matter, and how this matter worth searching for is Jesus, we will focus on two Old Testament kings in particular to find Him. Though Saul will have a great part to play, David and his son Solomon will be our treasure map. After inspecting the lives of these kings, Jesus Himself will be our great reward.

Additionally, David and Solomon provide a clear connection to Christ and His church. Like David was a man of war, so was Jesus. Jesus fought the war so we could be at rest. How did Solomon inherit the kingdom? By being born into it! He was born into a kingdom of peace due to his father David's labor. Likewise, we inherited a kingdom without end through being born again on behalf of Jesus' finished works. This book will reveal our inherited rights as not only kings, but most importantly, as sons.

Even if you already have a great perspective of God, this book will only improve it. As Jesus becomes more evident within the Old Testament, so will our confidence in His ways become greater. Even the "inconsistencies" in the Bible will prove to have pointed to His goodness all along. Jesus Christ, the same yesterday, today, and forever (Hebrews 13:8).

1

Concealed Glory

"While ye have light, believe in the light, that ye may be the children of light. These things spake Jesus, and departed, and did hide himself from them." (John 12:36)

In this first and foundational chapter, *Concealed Glory*, we will cover the "coverings" of Christ. That is, His flesh and His words. The veil of Moses and the parables Jesus spoke will be the two main focal points used to accomplish this. In doing so, we will gain a tremendous appreciation for the regard He places on man's free will.

One of the greatest gifts God has given to man is his free will. One of God's greatest gifts in return is for man to freely choose Him.

Jesus has not hidden the treasures of the kingdom *from* us but *for* us. He has concealed aspects of His glory and facets of His divine nature for those who would seek for Him alone. He has hidden Himself with the intent of being discovered.

"But we speak the wisdom of God in a mystery, even the hidden wisdom, which God ordained before the world unto our glory." (1st Corinthians 2:7)

"To whom God would make known what is the riches of the glory of this mystery among the Gentiles; ***which is Christ in you****, the hope of glory." (Colossians 1:27) (emphasis mine)*

Jesus came to reveal the mystery of the kingdom: *Himself*!

"...Because it is given unto you to know the mysteries of the kingdom of heaven..." (Matthew 13:11)

What is a kingdom without a king? ...Jesus came to reveal the reason for heaven!

Up until Christ's showing, man lived in wonder of the things concerning the kingdom of God. Throughout each generation, prophets and holy men of God spoke of the mighty Redeemer to come... yet only in part. Even when strung together, each prophetic portion still left many questions unanswered.

> *"Which none of the princes of this world knew: for had they known it, they would not have crucified the Lord of glory" (1st Corinthians 2:8)*

Nevertheless, from God's perspective, the plan was clear from the start. Each prophet and prophesy, each psalmist and song, each king and priest: each account was clearly purposed. All converging one glorious day as Mary confessed, "*Be it unto me according to thy word.*" (Luke 1:38). Thirty years later, John the Baptist proclaimed, *"Behold! The Lamb of God which takes away our sin!"* (John 1:29).

Behold... This, my brothers and sisters will be the vital concept addressed: the choice to behold Him or not. Our sin remains if not beholding Him. This is how there could be a disciple of Christ and an enemy of His in the same crowd, hearing and seeing two different things. Some may have seen but neglected to truly behold. Some may have heard but refused to take His words to heart. Some walked away, yet in their sin. Be that as it may, the choice was theirs.

See, access to the kingdom of God is by invitation only. The desire to enter is the prerequisite, and the finished work of Christ is the door in which we walk through. Christ has invited *all* to enter! Unfortunately, there are those unwilling to answer His knock.

Have you ever heard the statement, *"Jesus is a gentleman; He won't barge in, He'll knock first?"* This is the power and humility of God: though He could easily overpower the dark and locked hearts of men, He humbly regards the decision to let Him in or not.

> *"Behold, I stand at the door, and knock:* ***if any man hear my voice, and open the door,*** *I will come in to him, and will sup with him, and he with me." (Revelation 3:20) (emphasis mine)*

"Knock, knock..."

Allow this statement to provide some perspective regarding this chapter's intention: the parables of Christ are as the knock to the door of men's hearts.

The Expanse of Christ

Before delving deep into Jesus' parables, it is important to first address the manner the Lord related to mankind by coming in His flesh. The lengths He traveled to identify with us was unfathomable. I will try my best to use an earthly example. In turn, we will achieve a greater perspective when addressing the concealment of Jesus' words.

I heard this analogy of the Lord coming to earth from a highly respected Bible teacher. It brought tremendous clarity concerning the magnitude of God. Now, imagine for a moment you find yourself on a boat in the middle of the sea. In whatever direction you set your gaze, all that is seen is unending ocean. No shore in sight!

Now picture reaching down and scooping a glass full of water and placing it on board the ship. In essence, you would have a bit of this massive ocean in containment. Importantly, the molecular structure of the water would not have changed, but only restricted to the glass you used to fill it with. So was the vessel of the flesh of Christ! Jesus, while in His flesh, was the grandness of Almighty God restricted to an earthly vessel.

Nevertheless, this example is far from comparable. The waters, and moreover, the universe... *fits in the span of His hand*!

> *"Who hath measured the waters in the hollow of his hand, and meted out heaven with the span, and comprehended the dust of the earth in a measure, and weighed the mountains in scales, and the hills in a balance?" (Isaiah 40:12)*

Consider this: how could we relate to an ant? How would they not be crushed under our feet when trying to associate with them? Though we may have intended to advance the ant kingdom, we would have wound up only destroying them in the process. We would have simply overwhelmed them.

For God to have related to man, He could not have possibly come in His true form. We would have been crushed by the weight of His glory.

Concerning Jesus' convergence on earth, His coming in the flesh was the first covering of God. He was then covered by the Father for thirty years before stepping out into His assignment.

Just take a moment to reflect on *some* of what Jesus put aside in coming to earth. Not only did He give up the glory of heaven, but He gave His life altogether through a bloody and gruesome crucifixion. He was betrayed by one of His own and forsaken by His closest friends. Leading up to His innocent murder, the Creator subjected Himself to earthly laws, authorities, and even human parents. He lived a life of perfect love yet was despised, mocked, and rejected. Nevertheless, for the joy set before Him, He patiently triumphed. He conquered death!

For us.

Bearing the incomprehensible concept of God coming to earth in mind, let us now discuss the necessity of His parables and how and why they relate to us today.

Speak Plainly Lord!

Jesus' disciples questioned why He spoke in parables, and truth be told, I imagine you and I would as well.

They asked:

"Lord, why are you speaking in riddles? Why not speak plainly?"

His reply:

> *"...Because it is given unto you to know the mysteries of the kingdom of heaven, but to them it is not given...That it might be fulfilled which was spoken by the prophet, saying, I will open my mouth in parables; I will utter things which have been kept secret from the foundation of the world." (Matthew 13:11, 35)*

Jesus was the secret from the foundation of the world, but even in plain sight, He appeared to be hidden. His hidden mission, His hidden identity, His hidden path; the mystery of Christ was only revealed to those who found themselves alone with Him.

> *"But without a parable spake he not unto them:* ***and when they were alone****, he expounded all things to his disciples" (Mark 4:34) (emphasis mine)*

This statement is key: when they were alone with Him…

In public, Jesus' kingdom words were as water balloons or semi-transparent containers that harbored His true intent. Most could tell something was there on the inside but couldn't quite grasp it. Only those who sought Him afterward had these truths broken over their heads and were drenched.

What brilliance and manifold wisdom of God! Truly, the way Jesus spoke initiated a genuine response. On the one hand, you had those who wanted more, and on the other, those who wanted nothing to do with Him. There were those who sincerely asked: "Master, what are you really saying?" and those who chose not to question any further.

Interesting to note… isn't it peculiar how Jesus, the "Teacher of teachers," had His followers constantly questioning what He truly meant? Surely a good teacher would do everything possible for their students to understand what they were saying, right?

Isn't that the point?

Perhaps you were a good teacher, and your concept wasn't being grasped. Wouldn't you strive to make it as clear and concise as possible? Well, it doesn't appear to be the case with the greatest teacher of all! At times, it seemed He would almost go out of His way to make things harder to understand!

> *"These things said he in the synagogue, as he* ***taught*** *in Capernaum. Many therefore of his disciples, when they heard this, said,* ***This is an hard saying****; who can hear it? When Jesus knew in himself that his disciples murmured at it, he said unto them,* ***Doth this offend you****?" (John 6:59-61) (emphasis mine)*

He hardly explained Himself when saying something hard to be accepted. We may have apologized for their misunderstanding… but Jesus appeared to encourage it! Continuing with Jesus' speech, we find a clue as to why He made it so difficult:

> *"...Doth this offend you? What and if ye shall see the Son of man ascend up where he was before? It is the spirit that quickeneth; the flesh profiteth nothing: the words that I speak unto you, they are spirit, and they are life.* ***But there are some of you that believe not. For Jesus knew from the beginning who they were that believed not, and who should betray him.****" (John 6:61-64) (emphasis mine)*

...There are some of you that believe not. This was a major reason behind His concealment.

Hardened Hearts

> *"I will open my mouth in a parable: I will utter dark sayings of old." Psalm 78:2*

The "Parable of the Sower" can be found in the book of Matthew, Mark, and Luke. In Matthew and Mark specifically, there is a great exposition of the potency of Jesus' words. They were so pure in fact, He *had* to conceal them through parables. Follow along with me concerning the mystery and complexity of Jesus' manner of speech.

> *"And he said unto them, Unto you it is given to know the mystery of the kingdom of God:* ***but unto them that are without, all these things are done in parables****: That seeing they may see, and not perceive; and hearing they may hear, and not understand;* ***lest at any time they should be converted, and their sins should be forgiven them.****" (Mark 4:11, 12) (emphasis mine)*

Wow! What a profound statement from Jesus: *that their sins should be forgiven.* Now wait a second. Isn't that precisely what He came to do? To die for the sins of the *whole* world? If you're anything like me, this statement may have, or may still, confuse you. Would you agree it seemingly contradicts the nature of God?

"Jesus! The Lamb of God who died for the sins of the whole world! (1st John 2:2) *Well…* not really the *whole* world… everyone except for those referred to in Mark 4, of course." *Well…* except for what! There is only one exception: context. God is not the author of confusion nor the God of contradiction. So, let's consider the context.

Before coming to earth, Jesus knew there were those who would hate Him and those who would love Him. He knew some would embrace Him as the Way, the Truth, and the Life, and how some would rather seek to trip, catch, and deliver Him over to death.

> *"...the scribes and the Pharisees began to urge him...Laying wait for him, and seeking to catch something out of his mouth, that they might accuse him." (Luke 11:53, 54)*

> *"And when the chief priests and Pharisees* ***had heard his parables,*** *they perceived that he spake of them...And Jesus answered and* ***spake unto them again by parables****...Then went the Pharisees, and took counsel how they might* ***entangle him in his talk."*** *(Matthew 21:45, 22:1, 15) (emphasis mine)*

Some were more interested in ridding Him from the earth than accepting Him as Lord. Some weren't for Him from the beginning, and Jesus knew the hearts of all men. This is not to say those mentioned couldn't be saved or were "unworthy" of salvation, but only to regretfully say some simply didn't want it.

All that to say...

Consider it in this light: had Jesus spoken openly when amongst the multitudes, instead of in parables, the dark hearts of the men who didn't want Him wouldn't have stood a chance against the brightness and the glory of His Word! He would have blown the doors of their hearts off the hinges! The same God who spoke, *"Let there be light,"* would have given absolute light to the dark hearts of those who didn't even want it.

Irresistible

> *"And the earth was without form, and* ***void;*** *and* ***darkness was upon the face of the deep****, And the Spirit of God moved upon the face of the waters." (Genesis 1:2) (emphasis mine)*

There was a *void* in the earth; it was missing something. It was missing the spoken Word of God… it was missing His light!

"And God said, Let there be light: and there was light." (Genesis 1:3)

The formless earth had no choice but to obey the Word of God. The darkness upon the face of the deep, and the void within the earth, were filled with His light. In like manner, the void within the dark hearts of men would have been filled by the limitless power of His spoken Word: "*Let there be.*"

Just as the earth had no other option when hearing God's Word, so would it have been for man. However, it would not have been out of willing obedience or genuine desire, for that matter: it would have been irresistible. Now, rather than Him saying let there be light… He desires *us* to say let there be light!

Had Jesus spoken without restraint, *all* who heard would have been irresistibly regenerated. Their will, and their hearts, would have been easily overtaken. His unrestrained word would have cleansed them by default and converted them against their heart's desire (Mark 4:11, 12). They wouldn't have had the choice to answer His knock.

This is what Jesus meant by converting them and forgiving them of their sins! Not that He didn't *want* to convert them. On the contrary, He wills that none would perish, but that all would come to repentance (2nd Peter 3:9). So, how is this seeming contradiction rectified?

He simply wanted them to want Him, therefore He knocked.

Though an unjust comparison, relating this to when the soldiers sought to detain Jesus in Gethsemane and fell back onto the ground after Christ said, *"I am He,"* would be appropriate… but in no wise sufficient. For had He spoken in all His power and majesty, they wouldn't have been able to get back up. Likewise, had Jesus spoken *"Let there be light"* in the same manner as He did in the beginning of creation… nothing could have stopped it.

The soldiers falling after experiencing a minuscule fraction of God's power reminds me of the three disciples catching a glimpse of God's glory beyond the veil.

The Veil

> *"And he said, Thou canst not see my face: for there shall no man see me, and live." (Exodus 33:20)*

Consider Peter, James, and John upon the mount of transfiguration (Matthew 17, Mark 9, Luke 9). They became heavy with sleep when Jesus' clothing and countenance shone in splendor. Even then, He was still in His flesh. Truly, it wouldn't have been only drowsiness for the disciples, but death! Without question, the frames of men created from dust would have collapsed from the weight of God's true unveiled glory. Interestingly, Moses also appeared at this encounter.

Behold the meek and mighty Moses, the friend of God! Yet even he was told he would have died if seeing God as He truly is. Therefore, the Lord revealed only a portion of Himself (Exodus 33:20-23). The Father covered Moses with His hand as He passed by. He then spent 40 days with God on a supernatural fast *(no food and no water!)* Afterward, Moses' face shone, insomuch he wore a veil to speak with the multitudes!

Before Jesus stepped out into His public ministry, He also fasted before the Lord for 40 days.

> *"And it came to pass, when Moses came down from mount Sinai with the two tables of testimony in Moses' hand, when he came down from the mount, that Moses wist not [wasn't aware] that **the skin of his face shone** while he talked with him. And when Aaron and all the children of Israel saw Moses, behold, the skin of his face shone; and they were afraid to come nigh unto him." (Exodus 34:29, 30) (emphasis and brackets mine)*

After spending time alone with God on the mountain, Moses came down, shining with the words of God in his hands! The people being afraid to go near him greatly depicted what it would have been like if Jesus came in His shining glory with the holy words of God uncovered.

> *"And till Moses had done speaking with them, he put a vail on his face. But when Moses went in before the LORD to speak with him, he took the vail off, until he came out. And he came out, and spake unto the*

children of Israel that which he was commanded. And the children of Israel saw the face of Moses, that the skin of Moses' face shone: and Moses put the vail upon his face again, until he went in to speak with him." (Exodus 34:33-35)

Moses covering his face when addressing the multitudes was an awesome foreshadowing of Jesus' earthly ministry. See, Jesus also wore a veil… His flesh! Like Moses, Jesus wore a veil so not to blind the people. Not only were Jesus' words hidden through parables so not to overtake the hearts of men against their will, but so was His glory concealed through His flesh so not to kill them!

What's also significant is how Moses would take the veil on and off, depending on to whom he spoke. The scripture says that he would speak with God without the veil and then speak with the children of Israel with it. It also appears he seemingly slipped and began to speak with the children of Israel without the veil upon his face:

"...And he came out, and spake unto the children of Israel that which he was commanded. And the children of Israel saw the face of Moses, that the skin of Moses' face shone: and Moses put the vail upon his face again. (Exodus 34:34, 35)

I believe this occurrence directly correlated to the mount of transfiguration, where Peter, James, and John saw Jesus without the veil. As the children of Israel saw Moses for a moment without his veil, so did the three disciples catch a glimpse of Jesus shining without His.

(Though Jesus was still in His flesh, because no man can see God at any time and live, the disciples saw God's glory beyond the veil. Amongst many things, Jesus' flesh was as a divine buffer, enabling men to see God. As the Father covered Moses to safely witness a glimpse of His glory... so was Jesus, God's outstretched Hand, concealed for mankind to catch a glimpse of God's glory!)

Moreover, men and women of Christ's day at times would also catch a glimpse of the ark beyond the veil and cry, *"You are the Christ, the Son of the living God!"* Or, *"Hosanna in the highest!"* Surely, they were seeing past the flesh of Jesus.

The veil in the temple separated man from God; however, the veil of Jesus' flesh enabled men to see the glory of God through Christ.

Not only were "common" people able to see the ark through Jesus' flesh, but they could also touch it! God wanted to be touched, and He wanted to be seen! However, before Christ, there wasn't any way for man to do so physically.

To that point, consider Uzzah:

> *"And when they came to Nachon's threshingfloor,* ***Uzzah put forth his hand*** *to the ark of God,* ***and took hold of it****...And the anger of the LORD was kindled against Uzzah, and God smote him there for his error; and there he died by the ark of God." (2nd Samuel 6:6, 7)*

Uzzah reached out to touch the ark of God and died! Truly, no flesh can glory in His presence.

Consider the Bethshemites who gazed inside the ark:

> *"And the Levites took down the ark of the LORD...And he smote the men of Beth-shemesh, because they had* ***looked into*** *the ark of the LORD..." (1st Samuel 6:15, 19)*

Nevertheless, through Christ, men and women beheld and touched the ark and lived!

> *"And the Word was made flesh, and dwelt among us, (and we beheld his glory, the glory as of the only begotten of the Father,) full of grace and truth." (John 1:14) (emphasis mine)*

> *"That which was from the beginning, which we have heard, which we have seen with our eyes, which we have looked upon, and our hands have handled, of the Word of life." (1st John 1:1) (emphasis mine)*

God wanted to be seen and handled. Therefore, like Moses, God covered Jesus so men could behold His glory. Hallelujah!

With that said, Jesus' earthly ministry greatly relates to us today. Consider the Bible: through God's Word, we can handle and behold His glory!

Furthermore, like Jesus was seemingly hidden in plain sight, so is the Word of God. It doesn't jump off the shelf and force one to open it, nor does it blind one with its light and demand repentance. Though the priceless Bible is the answer to man's dilemma, it is often glanced over as foolish. Even so, the Lord longs for this world to see Him as He truly is.

Similarly, today, some may see the Bible as a parable in and of itself. Perhaps hard to understand or, in many ways, confusing. This is because it has a cover… it is God's concealed glory! Because they don't have Christ, the world cannot grasp the Bible. However, by God's amazing grace, we can! Therefore, we must abide in the Word of God, so the Word of God can live through us. Jesus wants to continue His redemptive ministry through us. We are living epistles read of all men (2nd Corinthians 3:2). We must live and preach the Gospel so that the Word may continue to knock at the door of men's hearts.

"...which is Christ in you, the hope of glory." (Colossians 1:27)

Pure Love

If not a genuine choice, is it genuine love?

Concluding our discussion thus far (regarding Christ's pursuit of humanity), consider these questions in closing.

Is it pure love if a woman doesn't have a pure choice? Would it not be an arranged marriage at best? Doesn't the woman have the chance to say yes or no when the man asks for her hand in marriage? If not, is it genuine love?

Now, does God know the hearts of all men? Of course! Does God have the right to reveal as He wills? Without question! Nevertheless, catching a glimpse of God's meekness and character causes us to appreciate what love truly is: It is that of selflessness. It is that of sacrifice. It is that of choice. *Truly*, His love was displayed on the cross. His love was demonstrated without condition *before* any reciprocation. He didn't wait for us to be worthy of it! His death on the cross was His proposal. We are the "women" who now say yes or no. Though He knows He's all that mankind needs, He accepted the inevitability of being rejected. He counted the cost for all who would consent to His call.

I can't help but consider the story of King Midas. Everything he touched turned into gold. If we can relate Jesus to King Midas for a moment, He had to wear a glove to stop everything He touched from becoming gold. Unfortunately, He knew some would rather the rust.

Jesus, *the Seed,* had to protect His Word while in public (conception occurs from intimacy in private) because everything reproduces after its kind. Now, with all due reverence unto the Lord, had He not protected Himself (or rather, protected those from Himself if they didn't genuinely want Him), He would have impregnated many with His Holy Word, who may have not consented.

Make no mistake: heaven will be filled with those who wanted Jesus, and hell will be filled with those who did not. Likewise, no one will be in heaven against their own will.

Therefore, let us choose this day whom we will serve. Knowing this: when we *choose* to get alone with the Word… *let there be light!*

> *"How that by revelation he made known unto me the mystery; (as I wrote afore in few words, Whereby, when ye read, ye may understand my knowledge in the* ***mystery of Christ****)." (Ephesians 3:3, 4) (emphasis mine)*

2

Death, Burial and Resurrection

"...whereby Jonathan knew that it was determined of his father to slay David." (1st Samuel 20:33)

When my siblings and I were children, my parents would hide plastic eggs around the house for us to find on Easter morning. Most had candy within them, some had coins, and some even had a dollar... but only one of these eggs had a five-dollar bill. The five-dollar egg wasn't the one that was placed for all to see easily, but it was hidden in the least expected spot.

Due to the difficulty of finding this egg, our parents would often help by saying, "cold... cold... warm... warmer... hot!" as we approached its vicinity. Now, in order to find this treasured egg, we had to listen to those who knew where it was hidden. See, the Holy Spirit will enable us to find the most valuable mysteries of Christ within His Word. He will lead us to Jesus so long as we are listening.

Now that we've begun our journey focusing on the King of kings Himself and the reason for His concealment, let us continue along this train of thought in our pursuit of Christ through another biblical king. King David is a prime example. Studying some of David's life will undoubtedly reveal God's concealed glory.

As mentioned in the preface, Jesus' death, burial, and resurrection can be found in the first book of Samuel. This is over 1000 years prior to Christ's arrival! Upon reading, you will surely conclude that no man could have had the foreknowledge, nor the wisdom, to have so perfectly penned this glimpse of the Savior to come. God alone, in majestic and glorious fashion, hid this gospel for the honor of His kings to discover... in three consecutive chapters, nonetheless.

Chapter 20 of 1st Samuel

The Plan

This gospel commences with David raising his concern to Jonathan, King Saul's son, about the king's intentions toward him. Now, Jonathan was not convinced that his father sought to kill him. However, David was.

He said:

> *"...but truly as the LORD liveth, and as thy soul liveth, there is but a step between me and death." (1st Samuel 20:3)*

For this cause, they conceived a plan to reveal the king's will and made a covenant with each other. Jonathan swore that he would not deceive David, and David swore he would not kill Jonathan nor cut off his household after becoming king.

> *"...for thou hast brought thy servant into a covenant of the LORD with thee: notwithstanding,* ***if there be in me iniquity, slay me thyself; for why shouldest thou bring me to thy father?****" (1st Samuel 20:8) (emphasis mine)*

Astonishingly, Jonathan knew David was to reign over Israel in his father's stead (1st Samuel 23:17). Jonathan, the eldest son, was the successor to the throne! He could have easily deceived him if there was any jealousy or bitterness in his heart towards David. Nevertheless, Jonathan chose David.

On a side note: some would hesitate to give their friend their last stick of gum; perhaps they'd split it in half. Jonathan, however, submitted the whole kingdom unto David. The love he had for him was unfathomable. Supernatural, if you would.

> *"And Jonathan caused David to swear again, because he loved him: for he loved him as he loved his own soul." (1st Samuel 20:17)*

As Jonathan and David loved each other as one, so are the Father and Jesus One.

The following day, a ceremonial feast was held in Saul's house, and David's presence was required at the table. David would intentionally miss this dinner to have Jonathan witness his father's reaction. If he were missed, Jonathan would assure him that Saul's intentions were pure, but if he reacted maliciously, they both would know his life was truly in jeopardy.

To convey Saul's response, Jonathan would take a young boy along to shoot three arrows in an open field. If his father spoke well of David, he would then shoot the arrows and say, *"Gather them up and bring them back to me,"* thus signifying David was welcomed back. If Saul's response was contrary, after shooting, he would then proclaim, *"The arrows are beyond you!"* which would indicate David was surely his father's enemy.

On the first day of the feast, Saul remained silent upon noticing David's absence. He thought something evil had occurred to him. The following day he broke his silence and anxiously enquired of his whereabouts. With the plan set in motion, Jonathan explained how David attended a yearly sacrifice with his family in Bethlehem. This infuriated Saul, only to reveal his harbored hostility towards David!

> *"Then Saul's anger was kindled against Jonathan...* ***For as long as the son of Jesse liveth upon the ground, thou shalt not be established, nor thy kingdom.*** *Wherefore now send and fetch him unto me, for he shall surely die." (1st Samuel 20:30-31) (emphasis mine)*

Astounded, Jonathan questioned his father, *"Why should David die?" (1st Samuel 20:32).*

David was innocent.

> *"And Saul cast a javelin at him to smite him:* ***whereby Jonathan knew that it was determined of his father to slay David."*** *(1st Samuel 20:33) (emphasis mine)*

Consequently, Jonathan arose from the table enraged and shamed for his father's response. Clearly, Saul intended to kill him! I think it is safe to say that Jonathan was now convinced. If the king were to have his way, David would have been speared to the wall. In fact, Saul had already cast a spear at David!

> *"And Saul cast the javelin; for he said, I will smite David even to the wall with it. And David avoided out of his presence twice." (1st Samuel 18:11)*

Truly, there was One speared for us, there was One who was pierced.

The Lamb Slain Before Time

Before proceeding, I would like to touch on a few of these passages. For one, Saul said: *"For as long as the son of Jesse lives, your kingdom will not be established."*

Who is the son of Jesse? Well, at the surface, of course, it's David. However, as long as the Son of God *(Jesus)* lived during His earthly ministry… we, the church, would have no established kingdom. It would require His death!

> *"...Jonathan knew that it was determined of his father to slay David." (1st Samuel 20:33)*

Like it was determined of Jonathan's father to kill David, so was it determined of the Father to slay Jesus! This was always the plan!

In order to have a new life established in the kingdom, it required the son of Jesse (Jesus) to die.

Proceeding further, we find Jonathan and David reuniting after three days. The number three is extremely significant in the Bible and almost always refers to Jesus' death, burial, and resurrection.

> *"...that I may hide myself in the field unto the* ***third*** *day at even." (1st Samuel 20:5) (emphasis mine)*

> *"And I will shoot* ***three*** *arrows on the side thereof, as though I shot at a mark." (1st Samuel 20:20) (emphasis mine)*

> *"...David* ***arose*** *out of a place towards the south..." (1st Samuel 20:41) (emphasis mine)*

David "arose" to meet Jonathan on the third day. Jonathan may have shot three arrows *as though* he shot at a target, but the three nails that pierced Jesus to the cross surely hit its mark.

> *"And when thou hast stayed* ***three*** *days, then thou shalt go down*

quickly, and come to the place where thou didst hide thyself when the business was in hand, and shalt remain by the stone ***Ezel.****" (1st Samuel 20:19) (emphasis mine)*

The name, *Ezel*, means *departure*. Jesus would depart from this world to spoil the enemy on his own front. He would depart through death and strip the keys of hell and death from the devil. Hallelujah! Through His death, we have life!

A crucial part of this embedded story is the "lad" Jonathan took along with him to retrieve the arrows. The Bible says this young boy didn't know the plan that David and Jonathan surmised:

"But the lad knew not any thing: only Jonathan and David knew the matter." (1st Samuel 20:39)

See, only Jonathan and David knew this plan. This *lad* represents humanity and, moreover, all created beings. This young boy had no idea what was truly going on. Only the Father and Jesus knew the matter! Only Jesus knew that it was determined of His Father to kill Him for the ransom of the world. No one knew the plan until afterward.

"And all that dwell upon the earth shall worship him... ***the Lamb slain from the foundation of the world.****" (Revelation 13:8) (emphasis mine)*

The devil had no idea. Only Jesus and the Father knew.

"Which none of the princes of this world knew: for had they known it, they would not have crucified the Lord of glory." (1st Corinthians 2:8)

The Winepress

The story continues with Jonathan shooting the arrows beyond the young boy. David then learned of Saul's true intention.

"And as soon as the lad was gone, David arose out of a place toward the south, and fell on his face to the ground, and bowed himself ***three times****: and they kissed one another, and wept one with another, until*

David exceeded." (1st Samuel 20:41) (emphasis mine)

Here it is again! The purposed number three! Does this remind you of a similar account while Jesus was in Gethsemane?

> *"Then cometh Jesus with them unto a place called Gethsemane, and saith unto the disciples, Sit ye here, while I go and pray yonder...Then saith he unto them, My soul is exceeding sorrowful, even unto death: tarry ye here, and watch with me. And he went a little farther, and fell on his face, and prayed, saying, O my Father, if it be possible, let this cup pass from me: nevertheless not as I will, but as thou wilt...He went away again the second time, and prayed, saying, O my Father, if this cup may not pass away from me, except I drink it, thy will be done...And he left them, and went away again, and prayed the* ***third*** *time, saying the same words." (Matthew 26:36, 38-39, 42, 44) (emphasis mine)*

Jesus prayed three times in the garden of Gethsemane! As David bowed himself to the ground three times and embraced Jonathan, so did Jesus bow Himself to the ground and embrace His Father's will.

> *"...and wept one with another,* ***until David exceeded.*** *" (1st Samuel 20:41) (emphasis mine)*

When *David* (Jesus) exceeded and subjected His will unto His Father's, He accepted the predetermined plan of salvation. Not the three arrows of Jonathan, nor the spear of Saul missing its intended target, but the three nails and spear that surely hit its mark in Christ.

Selah.

We will now proceed with the following chapter and continue to unearth the glorious gospel of Christ within.

Chapter 21 of 1st Samuel

Three Days In The Deep

> *"For as Jonas was three days and three nights in the whale's belly;* ***so shall the Son of man be three days and three nights in the heart of***

***the earth.**" (Matthew 12:40) (emphasis mine)*

*"And said, I cried by reason of mine affliction unto the LORD, and he heard me; **out of the belly of hell** cried I, and thou heardest my voice." (Jonah 2:2) (emphasis mine)*

Though Jesus went to hell, I do not believe He suffered there whatsoever. I believe He went to Abraham's bosom and was separated from all torment. David prophesies this in the Psalm's:

"For thou wilt not leave my soul in hell; neither wilt thou suffer thine Holy One to see corruption." (Psalm 16:10)

Peter then referred to this prophecy when he himself was prophesying on the day of Pentecost:

*"Whom God hath raised up, having loosed the pains of death: **because it was not possible that he should be holden of it.** For David speaketh concerning him, I foresaw the Lord always before my face, for he is on my right hand, that I should not be moved: Therefore did my heart rejoice, and my tongue was glad; moreover also my flesh shall rest in hope: **Because thou wilt not leave my soul in hell, neither wilt thou suffer thine Holy One to see corruption.**" (Acts 2:24-27) (emphasis mine)*

With that said, let us continue along with David's journey into the temple.

"Then came David to Nob to Ahimelech the priest: and Ahimelech was afraid at the meeting of David, and said unto him, Why art thou alone, and no man with thee?" (1st Samuel 21:1)

After departing from Jonathan, David came to the house of God unto Ahimelech. He and his men were hungry and asked the priest for provision. Ahimelech responded:

"...There is no common bread under mine hand, but there is hallowed bread; if the young men have kept themselves at least from women." (1st Samuel 21:4)

What a profound statement in the context of extracting Jesus from these

Old Testament passages.

> *"And David answered the priest, and said unto him,* ***Of a truth women have been kept from us about these three days****, since I came out, and the vessels of the young men are holy, and the bread is in a manner common, yea, though it were sanctified this day in the vessel." (1st Samuel 21:5) (emphasis mine)*

Jesus spent three days in hell after His crucifixion. As David went into the house of God, having kept himself from women for three days, so was Jesus in hell, kept from *women* (His bride, the church) for three days. Jesus was kept from His church for three days, so we would never be separated from Him again.

Pertaining to the shewbread, it wasn't lawful for David to have eaten it. Jesus refers to this account:

> *"How he [David] entered into the house of God, and did eat the shewbread, which was not lawful for him to eat, neither for them which were with him, but only for the priests?" (Matthew 12:4) (brackets mine)*

David had tremendous prophetic insight into God's grace concerning the coming Savior, and even superseded the law at times, through a revelation of the cross.

> *...And the bread is in a manner common. (1st Samuel 21:5)*

David being kept from the women, *the church,* was a foreshadow of the true sanctification to come through Christ. What a prophetic declaration! This signified what Jesus, the Bread of Life, would accomplish. Jesus was the lawful King and High Priest who would make the holy bread common for all mankind to eat.

What transpired in 1st Samuel chapter 20 enabled David to eat this holy bread and to give to the men who were with him because of the foreshadowing of Christ's death. Due to Saul's determination to kill David, he was able to eat this holy bread three days later. This signified the predetermined plan of the Father through Christ by His death, burial, and resurrection… thus enabling all to feast on the Shewbread… Jesus!

At times, David seemed to operate as a king *and* a priest, which was not lawful. There was only One who could operate as such, and that was Jesus. That is the point exactly. King David foreshadowed the King of Kings and Priest of priests to come.

Only Jesus had the right to eat what the shewbread represented. The shewbread represented a sanctification process that only Christ Himself could have accomplished. No priest, nor king, could truly sanctify the church. Only the death, burial, and resurrection of Jesus could.

The Keys Of Hell And Death

> *"And David said unto Ahimelech, And is there not here under thine hand spear or sword? For I have neither brought my sword nor my weapons with me, because the king's business required haste. And the priest said, The sword of Goliath the Philistine, whom thou slewest in the valley of Elah, behold, it is here wrapped in a cloth behind the ephod: if thou wilt take that, take it: for there is no other save that here. And David said, There is none like that; give it me." (1st Samuel 21:8-9)*

What an awesome parallel to Jesus' stay in hell! For one, David went into the house of God without a sword yet came out with Goliath's. Also, when David first met Ahimelech, the scripture states:

> *"...and Ahimelech* ***was afraid at the meeting of David,*** *and said unto him, Why art thou alone, and no man with thee?" (1st Samuel 21:1) (emphasis mine)*

All things considered: Jesus brought fear into the enemy's camp upon arrival. David entered the temple unarmed yet exited with Goliath's sword. This sword was used to cut off the accuser of Israel's head. After having sunk a smooth stone into the giant's forehead, David used Goliath's own sword against him! This reminds me of Haman being hung on the very gallows he built to hang Mordecai on. His plan turned on his own head.

"For I have neither brought my sword nor my weapons with me, because the king's business required haste" (1st Samuel 21:8). The Father's business led Jesus to hang naked on the cross for all to see. He

entered hell unclothed and unarmed. Nevertheless, Jesus was *clothed*: He was the Father's outstretched arm, the right hand of His Righteousness! (Jeremiah 32:17, Isaiah 41:10) This was the Father's ultimate weapon: Jesus, our *Righteousness*!

David embracing Jonathan, knowing his death was determined, entering the sanctuary, and then leaving with the sword of the enemy leaves us with a most beautiful glimpse of Christ's salvation.

> *"I am he that liveth, and was dead; and, behold, I am alive for evermore, Amen; and have the keys of hell and of death." (Revelation 1:18)*

Chapters 20 and 21 of 1st Samuel portray the death and burial of our Lord and Savior, but chapter 22 depicts the reason we are alive today: His glorious resurrection!

Chapter 22 of 1st Samuel

The Captain Of Our Salvation

> *"David therefore departed thence, and escaped to the cave Adullam: and when his brethren and all his father's house heard it, they went down thither to him. And every one that was in distress, and every one that was in debt, and every one that was discontented, gathered themselves unto him; and he became a captain over them: and there were with him about four hundred men." (1st Samuel 22:1-2)*

Without coincidence, this account was written for the honor of kings to discover. What glory is God concealing? The glory of His Son Jesus Christ! It is God's glory, but our honor, to see Jesus within the living pages of His Holy Word.

> *"...and when his brethren and all his father's house* ***heard it,*** *they went down thither to him." (1st Samuel 22:1) (emphasis mine)*

When the house of David *heard* how he escaped, they all came unto him. Hallelujah! When we hear the good news of Jesus Christ and how He escaped the hold of death, having swallowed it in victory, we gather ourselves unto Him!

> *"...and he became a captain over them." (1st Samuel 22:2)*

David became their captain! Moreover, these men who gathered themselves unto David became his "mighty men." Some of them are accounted for in 2nd Samuel, chapter 23, detailing their amazing feats! These men who spent time with David became great!

> *"...but the people that do know their God shall be strong, and do exploits." (Daniel 11:32)*

Interestingly, these courageous men of David were those who King Saul overlooked. Also, what's notable about the beginning of David's reign was how he *gave*. Unlike Saul, who took, David was a giver:

> *And David perceived that the LORD had confirmed him king over Israel, for his kingdom was lifted up on high, because of his people Israel...So they brought the ark of God, and set it in the midst of the tent that David had pitched for it: and they* ***offered*** *burnt sacrifices and peace offerings before God...***And he dealt to every one of Israel***, both man and woman, to every one a loaf of bread, and a good piece of flesh, and a flagon of wine. (1st Chronicles 14:2, 16:1, 3)*

What a leader! David considered God's people as those who were to be provided for, not that they should have provided for him. To serve, not to be served. This is what set David apart from other kings. Moreover, we as leaders must follow the example of Christ:

> *"Even as the Son of man came not to be ministered unto, but to minister, and to* ***give*** *his life a ransom for many." (Matthew 20:28) (emphasis mine)*

What a leader! Jesus was the greatest giver of all! *"For God so loved that He gave..."* (John 3:16).

On the other hand, look at the leadership example set forth by Saul. Take note of all the times Samuel mentions how this king they cried out for would *take*:

> *"And he said, This will be the manner of the king that shall reign over you: He will* ***take*** *your sons, and appoint them for himself, for his chariots, and to be his horsemen; and some shall run before his chariots. And he will appoint him captains over thousands, and captains over fifties; and will set them to ear his ground, and to reap his harvest, and to make his instruments of war, and instruments of his chariots. And he will* ***take*** *your daughters to be confectionaries, and to be cooks, and to be bakers. And he will* ***take*** *your fields, and your vineyards, and your oliveyards, even the best of them, and give them to his servants. And he will* ***take*** *the tenth of your seed, and of your vineyards, and give to his officers, and to his servants. And he will* ***take*** *your menservants, and your maidservants, and your goodliest young men, and your asses, and put them to his work. He will* ***take*** *the tenth of your sheep: and ye shall be his servants." (1st Samuel 8:11-17) (emphasis mine)*

The flesh takes, but the Spirit gives. Now, there are many lessons to learn through the lives of these two kings, both good and bad, but let's conclude with something you may have not previously tied together. Let us consider King Jesus and the men whom He chose.

There were a few fishermen: *Andrew, Peter, James, and John;* A tax collector: *Matthew*. There was *Simon* the "Zealot," who was once concerned about overthrowing the Roman government. Of course, there was *Judas*, the thief. And the rest, well… their professions aren't even mentioned in scripture. What is the point exactly? The men Jesus chose would have been the last choice of most Rabbi's, let alone kings. See, Jesus didn't choose based on what these men could provide for Him, but rather what He could provide for them. He didn't *take* from them, but rather He *gave* to them!

If these men (Jesus' disciples) were in King Saul's day, they would have been overlooked! Saul only took what was best for himself:

> *"And there was sore war against the Philistines all the days of Saul: and when Saul saw any strong man, or any valiant man,* ***he took him unto him****." (1st Samuel 14:52) (emphasis mine)*

For this cause, David inherited the outcasts of Israel! David's men consisted of all those Saul had turned away. Those who weren't even considered by Saul, soon became the mighty men of a seemingly rebellious king, which was David. Does this sound familiar?

Jesus didn't choose the Pharisees. He didn't choose the "learned" men. He chose the outcasts, and He built them up to become His mighty men. He saw in them what the eyes of the world had cast away. Jesus, going against the grain by all worldly standards, and being a perpetual thorn in the sides of His critics, took a group of ignorant people and made them His elite fighting force. After spending time with Jesus, and specifically after His resurrection, these men were emboldened to turn the world upside down for His glory! The book of Acts could be read as the great exploits performed by those who knew Jesus! (Daniel 11:32, 2nd Samuel 23).

Now for us...

What a testimony, and what glory to God, for this to be said of us: "*They took note that these unlearned and ignorant people had been with Jesus*!" Selah.

> *"And every one that was in distress, and every one that was in debt, and every one that was discontented, gathered themselves unto him; and he became a captain over them." (1st Samuel 22:2)*

We were all indebted, distressed, and discontented... but hearing and accepting the good news that Jesus is alive has set us free! We gather ourselves unto Him and declare Him Lord over our lives! Jesus, the captain of our salvation!

> *"For it became him, for whom are all things, and by whom are all things, in bringing many sons unto glory, to make the* ***captain of their salvation perfect through sufferings.****" (Hebrews 2:10) (emphasis mine)*

3

The Innocent Struck

"And Nathan said to David, Thou art the man..." (2nd Samuel 12:7)

In what appears to be a tragedy, the story of David and Bathsheba's firstborn being struck with sickness, and dying, is in fact, the gospel of Jesus Christ. It is a story of hope concealed for the glory of God. As we begin to dissect these passages and place these events in the right context, we can clearly see the goodness of God in the midst of man's rebellion and sin.

Good

To preface our next topic, let us briefly address God's good nature. We must develop the right understanding of God's nature, or else we'll fail to see Him as He truly is... which is *only* good.

For instance, say you have a "good" friend. They have a consistent track record of honesty, integrity, and faithfulness. You've known them for many years, and their character has remained unquestioned. They are caring, loving, thoughtful, and selfless. What a friend!

Now, imagine being faced with a glaring inconsistency in their life. Perhaps a report appearing to contradict their integrity or an action completely opposing their normal behavior. Upon this discovery, would you quickly disregard the many years of uncompromised history? Would you begin to frame your entire outlook on your friend based on this one occurrence? Would you even spare them the benefit of the doubt?

Brothers and sisters, we have a Friend better than the best friend on earth. Even the best friend we have, whether accidental or intentional, will surely miss the mark at some point; and when they do, we'll quickly forgive them because we know who they truly are. The mistake they made doesn't line up with their consistent character. Friends, the Lord doesn't need forgiveness for what seems to contradict His nature. He hasn't made a mistake.

Oftentimes, we approach God without knowing if He wants us whole or not and consider: *"What about Job?"* We see Jesus healing the *multitudes…* but we can't seem to forget about this *one* righteous man who suffered with sickness. Jesus' track record consists of healing thousands upon thousands, yet we don't know if He will heal us because, well… *what about Job?* We tend to trust more in the stories that seem to contradict God's character rather than complement it. The book of Job is a story of the judgment of sin and sickness *Jesus* would take upon *His* righteous body. The book of Job is the antithesis of God's will, not the standard. Job's plight should beg the question, "*God, this is not normal…"*

My friends… *That's the point.*

Bear with me a moment while aiming to prove this a bit further. Allow me to propose a few questions:

Besides Abraham, how many men did the Lord ask to sacrifice their promised son?

Who amongst men did He ask to walk naked and barefoot for three years besides Isaiah?

Who besides Ezekiel was commanded to eat man's feces? (However, after a brief conversation, the Lord obliged his request in eating that of an animal's…)

Who else bore wooden stocks on their shoulders and pleaded with rebellious Israel like Jeremiah? Who else wept due to Israel not believing His words?

Who else was swallowed up in the deep for three days like Jonah?

Who else…?

One occasion at a time, the Lord would raise up a prophet at a certain point in history. There could even be hundreds of years in between these instances. The length of time in between created a spectacle in and of itself! This contributes to the 400 years of silence before Christ's coming.

Now, if the Lord had asked thousands of righteous men to slay their sons each year or placed sickness and disease upon thousands of His righteous prophets… we can call this His normal behavior.

However, He didn't ask thousands. He only asked One.

The "contradictions" we find in the Bible are the antitypes of God's perfect will. The judgments the prophets walked out on earth would be the judgment the One man from heaven would carry out Himself. These few and far-between abnormal messengers sent from God all portrayed One.

Only One.

*"And Philip ran thither to him, and heard him read the **prophet Esaias**...In his humiliation his judgment was taken away: and who shall declare his generation? **for his life is taken** from the earth. And the eunuch answered Philip, and said, **I pray thee, of whom speaketh the prophet this? of himself, or of some other man**? Then Philip opened his mouth, and began at the same scripture, **and preached unto him Jesus."** (Acts 8:30, 32-35) (emphasis mine)*

...Of himself, or of some other man...

...Another man indeed!

This is the honor of kings to discover: God's good nature! Ultimately, (through erroneous doctrine, traditions of men, and misinterpretation), we have misunderstood the true nature of God.

With that said, the instance with David and Bathsheba's baby being struck with sickness and dying is no different. There is no limit to expounding upon the perfect track record of God and much more to discuss concerning Job and the prophets but let us focus on one event in particular: the innocent death of David's firstborn son in Jerusalem.

Thou Art The Man

The story begins with the prophet Nathan being sent unto David with an interesting parable. It would be beneficial to note the theme of the illustration:

"And the LORD sent Nathan unto David. And he came unto him, and said unto him, There were two men in one city; the one rich, and the other poor. The rich man had exceeding many flocks and herds: But

the poor man had nothing, save one little ewe lamb, which he had bought and nourished up: and it grew up together with him, and with his children; it did eat of his own meat, and drank of his own cup, and lay in his bosom, and was unto him as a daughter. And there came a traveller unto the rich man, and he spared to take of his own flock and of his own herd, to dress for the wayfaring man that was come unto him; but took the poor man's lamb, and dressed it for the man that was come to him. And David's anger was greatly kindled against the man; and he said to Nathan, As the LORD liveth, the man that hath done this thing shall surely die: And he shall restore the lamb fourfold, because he did this thing, and because he had no pity. And Nathan said to David, Thou art the man..." (2nd Samuel 12:1-7)

I will say this… I wouldn't want to have been David after receiving this rebuke from God. I'm certain he was cut to his core. This was the Lord's anointed! The sweet psalmist of Israel, the man after God's own heart! I can't begin to imagine the emotions welling within David… he seemingly threw it all away.

The prophet then delivered God's judgment:

"And David said unto Nathan, I have sinned against the LORD. And Nathan said unto David, The LORD also hath put away thy sin; thou shalt not die. Howbeit, because by this deed thou hast given great occasion to the enemies of the LORD to blaspheme, the child also that is born unto thee shall surely die. And Nathan departed unto his house. And the LORD struck the child that Uriah's wife bare unto David, and it was very sick." (2nd Samuel 12:13-15)

Astonishingly, David was not put to death for his sin. *The sure mercies of David...* (Isaiah 55:3). However, their innocent baby was struck with sickness and died seven days later in his stead. Wait a minute… David deserved to die! Why on earth would this baby suffer for David's evil? There is an inconsistency here… is He who is holy and just, also the killer of the innocent?

What did the baby have to do with it?

"David therefore besought God for the child; and David fasted, and went in, and lay all night upon the earth. And the elders of his house arose, and went to him, to raise him up from the earth: but he would not, neither did he eat bread with them. And it came to pass on the seventh day, that the child died..." (2nd Samuel 12:16-18)

At the surface, this appears to be one of the Bible's inconsistencies. At first glance, this seems to contradict the nature of God. How could God strike an innocent child? I can understand the enemy having place through sin… yet the scripture clearly states how the Lord did it:

"...And the LORD struck the child that Uriah's wife bare unto David, and it was very sick." (2nd Samuel 12:15)

Let's pause here momentarily to implement the proper context. Let's bring this story to justice by providing the right perspective. In order to accomplish this, we need to discuss David's lineage.

Six In Hebron

"And unto David were sons born in Hebron: and his ***firstborn*** *was Amnon, of Ahinoam the Jezreelitess; And his* ***second****, Chileab, of Abigail the wife of Nabal the Carmelite; and the* ***third****, Absalom the son of Maacah the daughter of Talmai king of Geshur; And the* ***fourth****, Adonijah the son of Haggith; and the* ***fifth****, Shephatiah the son of Abital; And the* ***sixth****, Ithream, by Eglah David's wife. These were born to David in Hebron." (2nd Samuel 3:2-5) (emphasis mine)*

Take note that David's six sons born in Hebron are mentioned in order. This passage is also repeated in First Chronicles:

"Now these were the sons of David, which were born unto him in Hebron; the ***firstborn*** *Amnon, of Ahinoam the Jezreelitess; the* ***second*** *Daniel, of Abigail the Carmelitess: The* ***third****, Absalom the son of Maachah the daughter of Talmai king of Geshur: the* ***fourth****, Adonijah the son of Haggith: The* ***fifth****, Shephatiah of Abital: the* ***sixth****, Ithream by Eglah his wife. These* ***six*** *were born unto him in Hebron; and there he reigned seven years and six months: and in Jerusalem he reigned*

thirty and three years." (1st Chronicles 3:1-4) (emphasis mine)

However, the passage found in First Chronicles differs from Second Samuel in that David's lineage is mentioned past Hebron, continuing throughout his reign in Jerusalem:

> *"These six were born unto him in Hebron; and there he reigned seven years and six months: and in Jerusalem he reigned thirty and three years.* ***And these were born unto him in Jerusalem; Shimea, and Shobab, and Nathan, and Solomon, four, of Bathshua the daughter of Ammiel."*** *(1st Chronicles 3:4-5) (emphasis mine)*

These two accounts reveal the gospel of Christ. Though buried, God's mercy becomes evident when applying the right perspective. What perspective, you may ask? A *good* one. Not a good perspective per se, but rather a perspective that *He* is good.

Now, consider the succession of David's sons. The six birthed in Hebron are mentioned in order: David's firstborn: *Amnon*; his second born: *Daniel*; his third: *Absalom*, and so on. However, when his four sons are mentioned by him and Bathsheba in Jerusalem, there is no specific order. The scripture simply states them all at once: *"four, of Bathsheba."*

This is without coincidence! Just like Paul mentions how it is *seed*, not *seeds*, plural (Galatians 3:16), concerning the promise to Abraham, so does this paragraph compare. Word placements, numerologies, and recurring patterns are significantly placed by the Holy Spirit to uncover the glory of Christ. It is written with divine specificity.

Firstborn In Jerusalem

We know the order of sons born unto David and Bathsheba accounted for in First Chronicles cannot be in succession, like David's lineage in Hebron, because Solomon is mentioned last. Solomon was the second son born unto David and Bathsheba, not the fourth. After the death of their firstborn, Bathsheba conceived Solomon:

> *"Then David arose from the earth, and washed, and anointed himself, and changed his apparel, and came into the house of the LORD, and*

> *worshipped: then he came to his own house; and when he required, they set bread before him, and he did eat...And David comforted* ***Bathsheba his wife****, and went in unto her, and lay with her:* ***and she bare a son, and he called his name Solomon****: and the LORD loved him. And he sent by the hand of Nathan the prophet; and he called his name Jedidiah, because of the LORD." (2nd Samuel 12:20, 24-25) (emphasis mine)*

Everything changed! For one, Bathsheba was first addressed as Uriah's wife (*rightfully so*) but is now mentioned as David's wife. Secondly, the Lord loved Solomon! Moreover, the prophet who once pronounced judgment upon the innocent child now declared a blessing upon the second born! Nathan also named him *Jedidiah*, which means "*beloved of the Lord.*"

Wait a second... We seem to be faced with another inconsistency here! This turnaround begs the question: *Could the Lord love this child and despise the other?* Although that appears to be the case, it simply cannot be. So, what really happened here? What was the difference between the two children?

See, David deserved to die for what he did. However, the innocent child took the judgment instead. Without coincidence, the child was the seventh-born son unto David (*six were first birthed in Hebron)* but the firstborn in Jerusalem. David's firstborn son in Jerusalem died in his place. The innocent child who hadn't sinned died for David's transgression.

The number *seven* represents *completion, perfection, and rest.* Jesus would be the innocent child who would take the sin of man upon himself, finishing His Father's work, making the way for the second-born sons and daughters to inherit the kingdom of God.

Like David's firstborn son in Jerusalem was slain by God, so was Jesus, the firstborn son, slain by the Father.

Solomon was the eighth-born son of David. The number *eight* represents *new beginnings*. Because of the death of the innocent one, Jesus, we have a new beginning! Also, to note, the name *Solomon* is translated from *Shalomah*, which derives from *Shalom*, which ultimately means *peace*. Though we deserved to die like David, the innocent One took death in our stead and, in turn, gave us peace.

Lastly, the parable Nathan delivered unto David was initially about a lamb. The sacrifice of the unblemished firstling of the flock was always a typology of innocence.

It's all about the Lamb.

> *"For he hath made him to be sin for us, who knew no sin; that we might be made the righteousness of God in him." (2nd Corinthians 5:21)*

Sin To Death

Before concluding this story, there is something I find difficult to accept to this day. David's response to hearing the news that Uriah was killed in the frontline of battle was totally ruthless. Not to mention, David made the order and sent him there to begin with.

> *"Then David said unto the messenger, Thus shalt thou say unto Joab, Let not this thing displease thee, **for the sword devoureth one as well as another**: make thy battle more strong against the city, and overthrow it: and encourage thou him." (2nd Samuel 11:25) (emphasis mine)*

This response from David is incredible. There is no remorse, pity, or realization of his evil. Just a nonchalant comment in regard to the man he just sent to his death. He basically said, *"Don't worry about this, don't be upset. The sword had its way with Uriah, just like it has its way with others."*

In speculation, I imagine that Saul would have had more sympathy than David here if it were his transgression! Moreover, if the handling of the matter in regard to falling with Bathsheba and killing Uriah was Saul's sin, I could have understood. Saul's heart was not perfect towards God, but according to scripture, David's was! What a transformation for the worse! In this case, Dr. Jekyll and Mr. Hyde have nothing on David here.

It just goes to show the treacherous power of sin. Like Adam was completely transformed by sin, so was David changed into an unrecognizable man. See, when it comes to sin, some Christians think they can master it, but on the contrary, sin masters them. Sin appeals to the flesh, and it comes at a great cost when indulging in it. It is never without consequence. Sin opens the door to the devil and gives him place. My brothers and sisters, we are to *never* give place to the devil (Ephesians 4:27). We only have one master now, and it is never to be sin.

> *"Neither yield ye your members as instruments of unrighteousness unto sin: but yield yourselves unto God, as those that are alive from the dead, and your members as instruments of righteousness unto God." (Romans 6:13)*

> *"Know ye not, that to whom ye yield yourselves servants to obey, his servants ye are to whom ye obey; whether of sin unto death, or of obedience unto righteousness?" (Romans 6:16)*

I may as well insert here the entire chapter of Romans 6! In regard to our baptism into Christ, Paul goes into depths by the Spirit in how we died to sin. He is considered *the* grace preacher when reading his epistles, yet he also makes it crystal clear on the repercussions of sin. We don't have an abundance of grace to continue in sin but rather to be free from it!

> *"What shall we say then?* ***Shall we continue in sin, that grace may abound? God forbid****. How shall we, that are dead to sin, live any longer therein? Know ye not, that so many of us as were baptized into Jesus Christ were baptized into his death?" (Romans 6:1-3) (emphasis mine)*

> *"Knowing this, that our old man is crucified with him, that the body of sin might be destroyed, that henceforth we should not serve sin.* ***For he who has died is freed from sin****" (Romans 6:6-7) (emphasis mine)*

Paul ministered on the grace of Christ in such a profound way that it often provoked the question: *"Am I free to do whatever I want?"* This question normally comes from one with a misunderstanding of grace altogether because those who do understand would always agree that grace is the ability *not* to sin. The power of sin has been crushed by grace, and we now have the ability to walk in absolute freedom.

Consider how Paul was adamant about setting the record straight concerning sin in Romans 6, yet in Titus 2, he reveals the proper instructor regarding it:

"For the grace of God that bringeth salvation hath appeared to all men, Teaching us that, denying ungodliness and worldly lusts, we should live soberly, righteously, and godly, in this present world." (Titus 2:11-12)

Grace is our teacher! Also, consider this passage in the way in which we walk in God's power and not that of sin's:

"This I say then, Walk in the Spirit, and ye shall not fulfil the lust of the flesh." (Galatians 5:16)

Obviously, David was not walking in the Spirit when he took Bathsheba unto himself. It wasn't when he saw her bathing on the roof that he fell. It was when he didn't rely on God's grace to take his eyes off her. See, for us today, grace teaches us how to do that!

...Teaching us that, denying ungodliness and worldly lusts... (Titus 2:12)

We need to rely on His grace in order to walk in power. Otherwise, sin is crouching at the door to take us out. Yet we need not fear sin! We are servants of righteousness and ambassadors of love! The power of sin has been destroyed. We now have a greater power. It's called righteousness. We are rightly standing with God by His grace.

"Being then made free from sin, ye became the servants of righteousness." (Romans 6:18)

Hallelujah!

In conclusion, 2nd Samuel provides a heartwarming justice. I love reading the account of David's mighty men, but the last verse in the chapter blesses me the most. After listing many of the feats each valiant warrior of David's accomplished, Uriah the Hittite is honorably mentioned last. If we know anything about the ways of God, we know that the first shall be last, and the last shall be first.

"These be the names of the mighty men whom David had... Uriah the Hittite: thirty and seven in all." (2nd Samuel 23:8, 39)

4

The Lord's House

"And he said unto me, Solomon thy son, he shall build my house and courts: for I have chosen him to be my son, and I will be his father." (1st Chronicles 28:6)

Now that we have introduced King Solomon into the picture, it seems fitting to expound upon his relation to us as kings today. Solomon's life has a tremendous correlation to the New Testament church. He is a figure of Christ, and his typology is revealed best when describing him as the earth Jesus would walk within versus the earth Jesus would walk upon. Jesus temporarily walked upon the ground of the earth to forever walk within the grounds of our hearts. Solomon will reveal this heavenly plan.

Solomon was divinely named after his gifted position. His name derives from the Hebrew word *shalom*, which means *peace*. Solomon inherited a kingdom of peace from his father, David. Today, The Prince of Peace has made His residence within Solomon's Temple… us! Like Solomon, we have inherited peace from our Father.

King Solomon will also transition us from beholding the Lord's glory to becoming the light for others to behold. Like the queen of Sheba traveled afar to meet Israel's glorious king, so will those scattered abroad be drawn to witness the majesty of God in Solomon's Temple. Foreigners from God's presence, exiles from the Lord and His ways, will undoubtedly experience His glory through us. That is, beyond the veil.

Additionally, the glory of the Lord filling Solomon's Temple was a type and shadow of the Holy Spirit filling His people on the day of Pentecost. This chapter will set the stage for the next: *Fill Me With Your Glory*! Beginning in Genesis and culminating in the book of Acts, God's perfect plan concluded. Though residing in us was His grand finale, the book of Acts continues still! Jesus said it was finished, yet through His people, His ministry lives on.

Man of War

Before elaborating on the rest Solomon inherited, it is vital to first address the wars of his father, David. This should clearly reveal the predetermined plan of the Father.

I used to think that David missed out on building the temple because of his fall with Bathsheba and the evil that ensued in killing her husband, Uriah. *Surely, if Moses missed the promised land because of his sin in striking the rock twice, then David stood no chance of building a holy temple because of his!* However, through study and revelation, I believe the plan of God is clear in scripture regardless of David's transgression. David isn't the focus to begin with.

> *"But God said unto me, Thou shalt not build an house for my name, because thou hast been a man of war, and hast shed blood." (1st Chronicles 28:3) (emphasis mine)*

Nevertheless, for clarity's sake, the obvious question should be proposed: was David disqualified from building because of shedding Uriah's blood? To answer this plainly, and according to instances that precede this account, David's fall had nothing to do with it. Though his actions were evil and tragic and cost him more than he could have imagined, God had *already* determined who would build His house beforehand. It wasn't because of David's sin!

1st Chronicles 28:3 is clear: *"...Thou shalt not build an house for my name,* ***because thou hast been a man of war****..."* This, regardless of David's sin, cannot be ignored. David was disallowed from building because of his profession. He was a man of war.

> *"But the word of the LORD came to me, saying,* ***Thou hast shed blood abundantly, and hast made great wars:*** *thou shalt not build an house unto my name,* ***because thou hast shed much blood upon the earth in my sight.****" (1st Chronicles 22:8) (emphasis mine)*

The better question (rather than imagine if he hadn't killed Uriah) would be this: would David have been able to build the house if he wasn't a man of war? This would be the more accurate question regarding David's denial from God to build. Nevertheless… still irrelevant! Not only would this question miss the glory concealed behind the Lord's statement altogether, but it would also prove to be a contradiction in and of itself.

For example, David wouldn't have been positioned to build if he hadn't killed Goliath from the start. In essence, he was promoted in the kingdom through bloodshed. Not to mention the countless lives that he and his men slew to ensure Israel's safety. He was in the position he was in as a direct result of his warfare. It was God's will!

Hence the predicament: David wasn't ever going to fulfill his desire to build! He wouldn't have been able to build if he wasn't a man of war, because he wouldn't have been positioned as king do so (because his bloodshed led him to the throne). On the other hand, he wouldn't be able to build if he was a man of war, because his profession would have disqualified him anyway! It seems cliché to say, "You can't have your cake and eat it too", but it fits. David couldn't have both. He couldn't have the kingdom through war, and the temple through peace.

That belonged to One.

The Lord's Temple

With that said, consider David and the prophet Nathan's interaction:

> *"And it came to pass, when the king sat in his house, and the LORD had given him rest round about from all his enemies; That the king said unto Nathan the prophet, See now, I dwell in an house of cedar, but the ark of God dwelleth within curtains. And Nathan said to the king,* ***Go, do all that is in thine heart;*** *for the LORD is with thee." (2nd Samuel 7:1-3) (emphasis mine)*

At this point (keep in mind, this was well before David's fall with Bathsheba), it was in David's heart to build a house for God. Now, Nathan had only witnessed the Lord prospering David's every move. Blessing after blessing, the Lord was behind it all. Due to this, Nathan spoke presumptuously when it came to building the temple. It is also important to note that Nathan didn't say, *"Thus saith the Lord... go and build..."*. He simply encouraged David to follow through in building because he believed God was inspiring it. Truth be told, God did generate that desire… but David presumed he would be the builder. That night the Lord used Nathan to tell David otherwise:

> *"And it came to pass that night, that the word of the LORD came unto Nathan, saying, Go and tell my servant David, Thus saith the LORD,* ***Shalt thou build me an house for me to dwell in?****...spake I a word with any of the tribes of Israel, whom I commanded to feed my people Israel, saying, Why build ye not me an house of cedar?...* ***Also the LORD telleth thee that he will make thee an house.****" (2nd Samuel 7:4-5, 7, 11) (emphasis mine)*

This is tremendous! I love how at the end of this passage, after David had it in his heart to build the Lord a house, God said He would build one for him! If I may interject, I find this response from the Lord funny. Truly, the Lord has a great sense of humor!

> *"...Shalt thou build me an house for me to dwell in?" (2nd Samuel 7:5)*

Imagine a child at the dinner table after the parents just prepared a hot meal for the family, and he turns around and says, *"Dad, Mom… I'm going to take care of you guys from now on. I'm going to provide for you now!"* I could imagine the parents thinking how sweet that statement was but also how unrealistic! This is what I picture transpiring between God and David here. The Lord was providing for David, and in turn, he was thankful and inspired to build. However, Jehovah Jireh is *our* provider, not the other way around.

> *"...Also the LORD telleth thee that he will make thee an house." (2nd Samuel 7:11)*

Alright, it's settled. Now we know the child will not be building a house for the Father, but the Father for the child. Yet, if we're following along, this still leaves us with a question: what did the Lord mean when He told David

He would build him a house? David was dwelling in a brand-new home:

> *"And Hiram king of Tyre sent messengers to David, and cedar trees, and carpenters, and masons:* ***and they built David an house****." (2nd Samuel 5:11) (emphasis mine)*

Without coincidence, and somewhat amusing, David was sitting in his house when the Lord told him He would build him one (2nd Samuel 7:1). Again, how funny! Obviously, David didn't need a new house. Now, this will come with some explanation, but I assure you that the house the Lord would build for David wasn't for David at all. It was for someone else. In fact, it was someone else. Though the Lord was speaking to David, He was simultaneously speaking through David to Jesus. In actuality, the Lord telling David He would build him a house was the Father assuring the Son how He would give Him (Jesus) a human body: "…but a body hast thou prepared me" (Hebrews 10:5). The House the Lord built through David's line was Jesus! It is more manifold than this, but David dying and Solomon building the temple truly refers to Jesus' dying and resurrecting us: His temple!

> *"Jesus answered and said unto them, Destroy this temple, and in three days I will raise it up." (John 2:19)*

Tear Down To Rebuild

> *"...I will set up thy seed after thee, which shall proceed out of thy bowels, and I will establish his kingdom." (2nd Samuel 7:12)*

The seed being set up *"after thee"* refers to us coming forth after the Seed (Jesus) was sown initially. Like Solomon came forth from his father David, so did we come forth from Jesus. Moreover, like Solomon received the kingdom from his father, so did we from God! The Lord established His own kingdom through Christ on the earth, and He passed it on to us as David did to Solomon! How did He accomplish this? He tore down in order to rebuild. He demolished His own house in order to rebuild another. More accurately, *many* others.

See, Jesus' perfect temple, *or house* being destroyed, made way for us to be perfected. We were condemned houses… the whole lot of us! Consider it this way: Jesus, the Perfect House, became condemned so that we, the condemned houses, could be restored. Not only are we habitable now, but we've been made suitable enough for the King of kings! What a restoration!

Consider this: what kind of home does a king live in? *A palace?... A castle?* Now, what kind of house does the King of kings live in? Well, that's simple; He lives in your house.

He lives in you.

You... rather, we... are His temple! We are "Solomon's Temple" at that! A glorious palace for His name's sake! We are the temples of the Living God (2nd Corinthians 6:16). Israel is waiting for Messiah to rebuild the temple… but Christ has already done it.

> *"He shall build an house for my name, and I will stablish the throne of his kingdom for ever." (2nd Samuel 7:13)*

Selah.

To briefly review, the Lord built a house *first* in Jesus. He was the house, *or the body the Lord prepared*, in order to prepare a place for us. However, due to sin, Jesus' house had to be condemned in order to restore us altogether.

> *"Forasmuch then as the children are partakers of flesh and blood, he also himself likewise took part of the same; that* ***through death he might destroy him that had the power of death****, that is, the devil." (Hebrews 2:14)*

Sin, like a high voltage wire feeding off the power lines into a home, surged through all our houses as well. Sin had absolute power over us. For this cause, Jesus redirected all the power of sin into His own body on the cross. In a sense, He became the conductor and was electrocuted to death. He was the burnt offering! We know that sin brought forth death, yet Jesus never sinned. Thus, the gospel is revealed through His temple being destroyed. Jesus' house was the *only* house worthy to stand, yet it was demolished. He was unrightly and unjustly condemned. Therefore, He alone has the right to restore each one of us. Through death, He destroyed the power of death (Hebrews 2:14).

He Shall Build My House

> *"Behold, a son shall be born to thee…He shall build an house for my name…" (1st Chronicles 22:9-10)*

Who is this son of David that would build God's house?

> *"…Jesus, thou son of David, have mercy on me." (Luke 18:38)*

Jesus of course!

> *"And when thy days be fulfilled, and thou shalt sleep with thy fathers,* ***I will set up thy seed*** *after thee, which shall proceed out of thy bowels, and I will establish his kingdom.* ***He shall build an house for my name****, and I will stablish the throne of his kingdom for ever." (2nd Samuel 7:12, 13) (emphasis mine)*

Though this prophecy was initially fulfilled through Solomon, *the son of David*, building the physical temple, it was primarily geared towards Jesus, *the Son of God.*

Jesus, the son of David, would build His church. A kingdom without end!

> *"Saying, What think ye of Christ? whose son is he? They say unto him, The son of David. He saith unto them, How then doth David in spirit call him Lord, saying, The LORD said unto my Lord, Sit thou on my right hand, till I make thine enemies thy footstool? If David then call him Lord, how is he his son?" (Matthew 22:42-45)*

David's "son," in regard to Jesus, was not his son at all. Though He was from David's line, He was not a mere descendant. He was the Son of God!

Along these lines, let's remember that the desire for us to build God's house is a good desire. God commended David for his desire to build. Nevertheless, Jesus is the builder. *He shall build my house (1st Chronicles 22:9-10)*. We as leaders must never forget that. Though we have this God-given desire to build His church, and though the pattern may be written upon our hearts as the Lord did unto David:

> *"Except* ***the LORD build*** *the house, they labour in vain that build it…" (Psalm 127:1)*

House of Rest

"For he is our peace..." (Ephesians 2:14)

Now, if you consider these two kings (David and Solomon) as figures of Christ, it is Jesus fulfilling both roles. David represented Jesus in this regard: David shed blood in order to give the kingdom over to his son Solomon. David's bloodshed enabled Solomon's rest. Without it, Solomon wouldn't have a kingdom at all. See, David was never going to build the house! His calling fulfilled was to hand the pattern over to his son Solomon. Solomon would fulfill David's desire.

Jesus, the true man of war, shed His blood through His death on the cross so that He might establish His kingdom on earth through us: Solomon's Temple.

"And, having made peace through the blood of His cross..." (Colossians 1:20)

We have rest from war because of Jesus' bloodshed! However, unlike David, in that he was disallowed from building the temple… Jesus now builds through us as Solomon: His church! Jesus was the only One who could do both, this glory was for Him alone! Like Abraham was told that his seed would inherit the earth, so is the Lord speaking to David. However, it's not about Abraham and his son Isaac, nor is it about David and his son Solomon… but only about the Father and His one and only Son Jesus.

"Behold, a son shall be born to thee, ***who shall be a man of rest****; and I will give him rest from all his enemies round about: for his name shall be* ***Solomon, [peace]*** *and I will give* ***peace and quietness*** *unto Israel in his days. He shall build an house for my name; and he shall be my son, and I will be his father; and I will establish the throne of his kingdom over Israel for ever." (1st Chronicles 22:9, 10) (emphasis and brackets mine)*

It is easy to tell that a development was built by the same builder because all the homes look the same, right? So it is with us! Jesus built us all to look the same! It is obviously not by our outward appearance but by what He built within. He framed and furnished the homes of our hearts with His peace. We are the houses of peace that provide rest to the weary traveler. As Solomon's name means peace, so are we the many "Solomons" that infiltrate this fearful and anxiety-ridden world.

> *"And if the house be worthy, let your peace come upon it: but if it be not worthy, let your peace return to you." (Matthew 10:13)*

This is precisely why Jesus called His disciples to let peace come upon a house or to let it return. They were, *as we are today,* homes of rest and peace commissioned to provide it for those who did/do not have it. The Lord establishes His kingdom on earth by offering one thing this world cannot: peace!

> *"Peace I leave with you, my peace I give unto you: not as the world giveth, give I unto you. Let not your heart be troubled, neither let it be afraid." (John 14:27)*

Peace, depending on the context, can better be defined as *harmony*. To be in perfect harmony, or agreement, with God. Imagine that we, as believers emanate a melody unto God through Jesus. Though we are all different instruments of Christ, we all create a perfect pitch together. A pleasing song consistently played unto our God. So, when we, being at peace with God, come to a house that is way off-tune… we can offer that house harmony with God.

The Father's Many Mansions

Regarding our discussion thus far, it is important to reconsider this familiar passage in John that we often quote concerning our desired mansion in heaven:

> *"Let not your heart be troubled: ye believe in God, believe also in me. In my Father's house are many mansions: if it were not so, I would have told you. I go to prepare a place for you. And if I go and prepare a place for you, I will come again, and receive you unto myself; that where I am, there ye may be also." (John 14:1-3)*

This may come as a shock to you… but the mansion we are hoping for in heaven is a current reality in the earth now. I do not intend to offend anyone, but the context is key regarding Jesus' statement.

The Strong's Concordance defines the word mansion as *a room, dwelling place, abode.* It is found only once in the KJV Bible and is the passage we just read in John 14. We have come to know the word mansion in our English vernacular as *"an enormous house."* If you were to do a word search right now on *mansion*, you would find it to say, *a large, impressive house.* Part of this definition rings true for us today because we certainly are an impressive house in the spirit. We are the temples of the Living God!

The problem is that we often put the things of the kingdom of God off to a later date. More specifically, when we die. To most Christians, the things of heaven are as far away as heaven itself. *"When I get to heaven, I'll finally have my mansion!"* Now, I'm not opposed to a literal mansion in heaven, but the conversation Jesus had with His disciples was not referring to a future event but rather to His up-and-coming resurrection.

A key to this passage is found within Jesus' opening statement: *"Let not your heart be troubled."* It is a matter of the heart! If you don't know by now, let me assure you, your *heart* is the dwelling place of the Lord. You are the abode of the Lord. In other words, you are the Lord's mansion.

> *"In my Father's house there are many mansions [rooms, dwelling places]" (John 14:2) (brackets mine)*

We are the current dwelling places (mansions) for God. Yes, you got it now! We are the many rooms that make up the kingdom of our God.

Prepare The Way

> *"And David said, Solomon my son is young and tender, and the house that is to be builded for the LORD must be exceeding magnifical, of fame and of glory throughout all countries: I will therefore now make preparation for it. So David prepared abundantly before his death." (1st Chronicles 22:5)*

Jesus made great preparation before His death while with His "young and tender" disciples, knowing they would soon inherit the kingdom of God.

> *"**For the kingdom of God** is not meat and drink; but righteousness, and peace, and joy **in the Holy Ghost**." (Romans 14:17) (emphasis mine)*

They would soon inherit the Holy Spirit! Jesus was preparing His disciples for heaven's invasion. Like David began to prepare abundantly before his death, in gathering resources and skilled laborers, so much more did Jesus prepare for a kingdom made without hands.

How exactly did Jesus do this? Like John the Baptist prepared the hearts of all who came to him through preaching and baptism for the Christ to come…so did Jesus towards His disciples through preaching and washing them with His Word to prepare them for the Comforter to come.

Jesus consistently taught them *"The Way."* He constantly ministered on how *"The kingdom of heaven is like this… The kingdom of God is likened unto a rich man… So is the kingdom of God, that a man would sow a Seed…",* He taught His disciples the things concerning Himself! They didn't/couldn't understand it while He was still on earth, but He knew they would soon understand it after His death. Like David prepared before his death for Solomon to inherit the kingdom, so was Jesus preparing by sowing His Word within the hearts of his followers before His.

> *"But the Comforter, which is the Holy Ghost, whom the Father will send in my name, **he shall teach you all things, and bring all things to your remembrance, whatsoever I have said unto you.**" (John 14:26) (emphasis mine)*

His resurrection would change everything! *David* would sow the seeds; *Solomon* would reap the harvest. Likewise, Jesus was preparing His disciples… His temple! The Holy Spirit, upon His infilling, would then bring all the words of Christ to their remembrance. All the heavenly principles, and mysteries of the kingdom of God that Jesus prepared by investing them within His disciple's hearts, were as the resources that King David abundantly prepared and gave over to Solomon.

Death and Exaltation

> *"Thus David the son of Jesse reigned over all Israel. And the time that*

he reigned over Israel was forty years; seven years reigned he in Hebron, and thirty and three years reigned he in Jerusalem. And he died in a good old age, full of days, riches, and honour: and Solomon his son reigned in his stead." (1st Chronicles 29:26-28)

Notice the word placement inspired by the Holy Spirit in this chapter. It is not without significance:

"Thus David the son of Jesse reigned over all Israel…thirty and three years reigned he in Jerusalem. And he died…" (1st Chronicles 29:26-28)

The 27th verse speaks of David's 33-year reign in Jerusalem… with the next verse saying, *"And he died."* Jesus, the Son of God, reigned over Israel through His death, at 33! Glory to Jesus! The gospel hidden once again in the Old Testament for his New Covenant kings to search out.

Consider the repercussions of David's death and how they pertain to Jesus':

"Then ***Solomon sat on the throne of the LORD*** *as king instead of David his father, and prospered; and all Israel obeyed him. And all the princes, and the mighty men, and all the sons likewise of king David, submitted themselves unto Solomon the king." (1st Chronicles 29:23-24)*

"Then ***sat Solomon upon the throne of David*** *his father; and his kingdom was established greatly." (1st Kings 2:12) (emphasis mine)*

Astonishingly, the scripture says Solomon sat upon the throne of the LORD… not the throne of David. This, of course, is not a typographical error! Without coincidence, Solomon (Jesus) sat upon the throne of the LORD.

"And the LORD magnified Solomon exceedingly in the sight of all Israel, and bestowed upon him such royal majesty as had not been on any king before him in Israel." (1st Chronicles 29:25)

Does this exaltation sound familiar?

> *"And being found in fashion as a man, he humbled himself, and became obedient unto death, even the death of the cross.* ***Wherefore God also hath highly exalted him, and given him a name which is above every name:*** *That at the name of Jesus every knee should bow, of things in heaven, and things in earth, and things under the earth." (Philippians 2:8-10) (emphasis mine)*

Solomon inheriting his father David's throne and being exalted far above any king before or after him, is the perfect foreshadow of Christ's exaltation to the throne.

> *"To him that overcometh will I grant to sit with me in my throne, even as I also overcame, and am set down with my Father in his throne." (Revelation 3:21)*

Jesus, the King of kings, inherited his Father's throne!

Jesus, the highly exalted One.

What's astounding is how David was still alive when Solomon sat on his throne:

> *"And also thus said the king, Blessed be the LORD God of Israel, which hath given one to sit on my throne this day, mine eyes even seeing it." (1st Kings 1:48)*

Like David, in a sense, "shared" his throne with Solomon on earth, (being that he was still alive when the kingdom was transferred) So are we seated in heavenly places with Christ! *"To him that overcometh will I grant to sit with me in my throne..."* (Revelation 3:21). Christ is alive, and He reigns through us on this earth; yet we're seated together in heavenly places (Ephesians 2:6).

> *"I am he that liveth, and was dead; and, behold, I am alive for evermore, Amen; and have the keys of hell and of death." (Revelation 1:18)*

Moreover, the symbolism of David being alive while giving his throne to Solomon speaks more specifically of the Living Father welcoming His Son into His throne. As we have thoroughly discussed in the preceding paragraphs, you are His temple, and your heart is His throne.

Finally, consider this verse here in Chronicles:

> *"Thus David the son of Jesse reigned over all Israel." (1st Chronicles 29:26)*

This is how the kingly line of David never failed! When Solomon sits on the throne of the LORD, truly, it is Christ succeeding through us, the New Testament kings and priests He has made us unto our God (Revelation 1:6).

> *"And moreover the king's servants came to bless our lord king David, saying, God make the name of Solomon better than thy name, and make his throne greater than thy throne. And the king bowed himself upon the bed." (1 Kings 1:47)*

> *"Verily, verily, I say unto you, He that believeth on me, the works that I do shall he do also; and greater works than these shall he do; because I go unto my Father." (John 14:12)*

These Old Testament accounts are written in the Bible to, firstly, reveal Jesus as His people discover His glory concealed and, secondly, encourage us in who we are now in Christ. It is not only to correlate these Old Testament patriarchs to Jesus or to receive revelation alone but to wholeheartedly grasp and apply all that Jesus has finished for us through His death, His burial, and His resurrection. The more we see Jesus' glory hidden in the Bible, the more we become like Him (2nd Corinthians 3:17, 18). Now, in our perfected spirit, we are just like Him (1st John 4:17, Hebrews 10:10, 14, 2nd Peter 1:1). Yet in our minds, we are slowly but surely catching up (Romans 12:2, Ephesians 4:23). The baptism in the Holy Spirit, and praying in tongues, will most assuredly hasten the process.

5

Fill Me With Your Glory!

God appeared unto Solomon in a dream, saying, *"Ask what I shall give you."* Notice this is a request from the Lord. It is a divine invitation. Like we discussed in the first chapter concerning the Lord knocking on the door of our hearts and not barging in, so it is regarding His complete takeover by the Holy Spirit. Although it is not by force, it is just that: *a takeover.*

He wants us to hand over our ways to walk in His. Truth be told, the keys to our house are not even ours to begin with. We are *His* house. We are the tenants; He is the owner! He took back the keys of hell and death and purchased us with His own blood. The least we can do is give him our whole heart. Consider this, He has the keys to every heart on the face of the earth, yet He still knocks.

> *"Except the LORD build the house, they labour in vain that build it..." (Psalm 127:1)*

If we are unyielded and are building anything apart from the Holy Spirit's leading, most assuredly, it is in vain. Especially when we are built up on contradicting doctrines and man-made traditions. As a result, the Word of God becomes ineffective. (Mark 7:13).

With that said, some, through erroneous doctrine, may say, *"Well, I guess it must not be God's will for me to be baptized in the Holy Spirit and to speak in tongues. Maybe I'm not meant to receive the gift."* This belief, or unbelief rather, is due in part to multiple "failed attempts" to receive the baptism of the Holy Spirit. They feel as if they got their "hopes" up one too many times, only to be seemingly let down. This type of thinking is detrimental for the believer and couldn't be further from God's will.

This chapter will address some common misconceptions and will prove that every good and perfect gift comes from the Father above... and He *never* changes His mind (James 1:17). In light of this, it is quite necessary to address the vitality of a believer being filled with the Holy Spirit right from the start. Indeed, it is the sum of the matter at hand:

You were made to be filled with God's Holy Spirit.

As much as there are many elements likened unto God's Word, such as *fire, water, seed, plow, sword, etc.*, so are we equated to different vessels of the Lord. Though we are called His house, or temple, we are also like waterways and wine bottles. We store living waters within the wells of our spirit and carry the new wine of the Holy Spirit for all who would care to drink.

Like a vessel was designed to be poured into, so were you formed to be filled by the Holy Spirit. In order for the world to taste and see that God is good through us, our cups must be filled and overflowing. In fact, this can only be done effectively from the overflow of your relationship with Him in the first place. Therefore, you *must* be filled!

> *"For all the wells which his father's servants had digged in the days of Abraham his father, the Philistines had stopped them,* ***and filled them with earth****." (Genesis 26:15)*

A dam can effectively stop a river. For this cause, the devil seeks to stop up the wells within us. We are the canals in which these mighty rivers of God flow through. Being that his kingdom is that of demonic fire, he is unrelenting in his efforts to hold back the water.

This is the enemy's plan: to fill our minds with the earth (or the world and its ways) and to cut off access to the well. Knowing this, we must only be filled with His Spirit and diligently guard our hearts against all else. He can't pollute the well itself (for this is our born-again spirit, in which the Holy Spirit Himself has placed a seal), but he can stop it up with earth.

A sidenote would be how Isaac strove with the enemy to regain access to his father Abraham's wells. Jesus made way for us to access the well of the Father that the devil had stopped up! To that point, I'm convinced there was a wellspring in the Garden that fed the four rivers which flowed out of Eden. This will be covered more thoroughly in the seventh chapter.

To that point, as the mouth must be careful of what's placed within it (for it enters the stomach and fuels the rest of the body, either building it up or slowing it down), much more must the ears and eyes be careful of what's placed within them, (for it enters the heart and either fortifies faith or compiles doubt and unbelief). How can one "take things to heart?" By way of the eye gate and ear canal. These are the entrances that scripture tells us to diligently keep:

> *"Keep thy heart with all diligence; for out of it are the issues of life." (Proverbs 4:23)*

To guard one's heart is to secure the eye and the ear gates, even as one would secure the gates of a castle. Truly, the contents of a castle are only as secure as the entrances are fortified. What good would all the treasure within be if the doors were left wide open? Hezekiah lost all to the Babylonian king after allowing him into his treasure house in the temple (2nd Kings 20:12-19). Unfortunately, some believers are complacent when it comes to keeping the doors of their hearts secured. Some are not as diligent as they ought to be when considering the priceless possessions held within.

Finally, adhering to these kingdom truths will therefore enable the Holy Spirit to flow without obstruction. His desire is this: to flood you with His glory… and, in turn, the rest of the earth!

> *"And blessed be his glorious name for ever: and let the whole earth be filled with his glory; Amen, and Amen." (Psalm 72:19)*

Fulfilled

This house was destined for the glory of God!

> *"Hitherto have ye asked nothing in my name: ask, and ye shall receive, that your joy may be full." (John 16:24)*

Truly, the greater works that we shall do is contingent upon asking the Lord to fill us with His glory. That said, take notice of the key word here in these following passages as Jesus is explaining the Father's heart for His sons and daughters.

> *"And I say unto you, **Ask**, and it shall be given you; seek, and ye shall find; knock, and it shall be opened unto you. For every one that **asketh***

> *receiveth; and he that seeketh findeth; and to him that knocketh it shall be opened. If a son shall* ***ask*** *bread of any of you that is a father, will he give him a stone? or if he* ***ask*** *a fish, will he for a fish give him a serpent? Or if he shall* ***ask*** *an egg, will he offer him a scorpion? If ye then, being evil, know how to give good gifts unto your children: how much more shall your heavenly Father give the Holy Spirit to them that* ***ask*** *him?" (Luke 11:9-13) (emphasis mine)*

Seeking, knocking, and asking for the Father's will (which is for the Holy Spirit to be given to those who ask) is clearly encouraged here by Jesus. He is revealing the Father's heart. He desires for us to *know* His will and to not settle until His will is accomplished. It is a matter of asking in faith because Jesus is not holding back from us!

Additionally, consider the context of Jesus' parable. He is mentioning a son asking his father for particular foods. These are natural things that are meant to sustain the natural body for a limited period of time. Soon the son will be asking for more the next time he is hungry. Contrariwise, notice the elements the father wouldn't give in place of what his son asked for: a stone, a serpent, and a scorpion. One is cold, inedible, and inanimate. The others bite and sting. These only hurt the body! These would never be given from the Father; these have the devil's name written all over them.

Jesus is clearly expressing the good gift towards His body: the Holy Spirit!

Though indirectly, Jesus also differentiates between the devil and Himself in this passage in Luke. He is indicating how He comes to give life and how the devil comes to steal it. Often believers ignorantly attribute tragedies to the Lord due to their misunderstanding of His sovereignty. God is sovereign, no doubt! Nevertheless… He is good. Once His goodness is seemingly contradicted, it is no longer a matter of His goodness and sovereignty, but the thief who comes to steal, kill, and to destroy (John 10:10).

Notice also how Jesus is mentioning elements that go *into* the body. More specifically, the belly. Natural food and drink will need to be replenished, but Jesus, being the bread and water of Life, will cause our bellies to be eternally satisfied. He is our source! This is precisely why Jesus said out of your bellies shall flow rivers of living water (John 7:37, 38). He was referring to Himself moving in! Of course, this has nothing to do with our natural stomachs but the hidden man of the heart. Though we need food and water to live, believers are sustained by the Word of God every day. Jesus spoke this scripture from Deuteronomy when the devil tempted him to turn a stone into bread:

> *"But he answered and said, It is written, man shall not live by bread alone, but by every word that proceedeth out of the mouth of God." (Matthew 4:4)*

Along these lines of our stomachs being filled, Solomon mentions a more distinguished element that enters into the body. He speaks of wine three times in his song when describing the love of God. This closely ties to receiving the wonderful gift of the Holy Spirit. What's also mentioned is how ointment, or perfumed oils, is something to be desired as well. The wine goes within, and the oil goes upon. This all points to the Holy Spirit.

> *The song of songs, which is Solomon's. Let him kiss me with the kisses of his mouth: **for thy love is better than wine**. Because of the savour of thy good **ointments** thy name is as **ointment** poured forth, therefore do the virgins love thee. Draw me, we will run after thee: the king hath brought me into his chambers: we will be glad and rejoice in thee, **we will remember thy love more than wine**: the upright love thee...How fair is thy love, my sister, my spouse! **how much better is thy love than wine**! and the smell of thine **ointments** than all spices!" (Song of Solomon 1:1-4, 4:10) (emphasis mine)*

Now, I cannot confidently speak on the Song of Solomon. These things are too wonderful for me. Nevertheless, I can confidently say how the book summarizes the intimacy of the Lord and His bride: His church. True to fashion, Jesus is clearly found throughout Solomon's song. It is the Song of Songs, after all! Without surprise, this book refers to a "King" and his wife. What better reason to rejoice!

In my previous book, *Out of Egypt, Into Promise*, I mentioned how Jesus' first miracle in Cana (when He turned water into wine) pointed towards his blood being poured out for us on the cross. I just want to highlight something right here. Natural elements, i.e., food, water, wine, ointments… they all point toward our bodies being satisfied with something greater. Like the spotless lambs were slain for the temporary covering of sin, so was Jesus slain for the complete remission. The precious lambs pointed towards something greater. Likewise, foods, wines and perfumes are reasons to momentarily rejoice… but the Holy Spirit is the complete fulfillment.

> *"Behold, my belly is as wine which hath no vent; it is ready to burst like new bottles." (Job 32:19)*

Though drunkenness is sinful and is never condoned, wine is mentioned in making the heart of men merry. More often than not it represents gladness and joy.

> *"A feast is made for laughter, and wine maketh merry..." (Ecclesiastes 10:19)*

> *"And wine that maketh glad the heart of man, and oil to make his face to shine, and bread which strengtheneth man's heart." (Psalm 104:15)*

For the topic of discussion at hand, being filled with new wine directly correlates to being filled with the Holy Spirit.

> *"And be not drunk with wine, wherein is excess; but be filled with the Spirit." (Ephesians 5:18)*

Consider the apostles. They and other believers were filled on the day of Pentecost, yet were mistaken for being drunk for good reason:

> *"Others mocking said, These men are full of new wine." (Acts 2:13)*

They were filled with new wine indeed! They were filled with joy unspeakable and full of glory (1st Peter 1:8). They were filled with the whole point of our bodies craving food and drink in the first place! Now, I don't believe they were staggering around like drunken men, but they were mistaken for being drunk, nonetheless. The crowd's mistakenness was more likely due to their boldness and manner of speech. They were acting besides themselves, as someone who is drunk would. One who is drunk would be bolder than normal. They do things they wouldn't normally do otherwise.

Case in point, the Holy Spirit empowers us to do what we couldn't have done on our own.

Empowered

Consider Jesus' disciples. They all forsook Him in His passion. From the garden to the cross, they all fled. Though John followed into the temple and was the only disciple at Calvary, he initially fled from Jesus as well.

> *"But all this was done, that the scriptures of the prophets might be fulfilled.* ***Then all the disciples forsook him, and fled.****" (Matthew 26:56) (emphasis mine)*

After the cross, however, they were totally different disciples. They were all empowered believers after being filled with the Holy Spirit; they were bold unto death! In fact, all besides John were killed shortly after Jesus' crucifixion. Though each one fled to preserve their lives initially, the baptism of the Holy Spirit enabled them to later lay theirs down. The Holy Spirit unquestionably transformed the disciples at Pentecost.

Consider this: had the disciples known what Jesus was doing at Calvary, they would have worshipped Him at the cross instead of fleeing! They would have been thanking Him for saving them, despite their possible executions. Then, *after* Pentecost, that is exactly what happened! They were found worshipping Jesus for the sake of His cross and were killed for their devotion.

The Holy Spirit emboldened them to become His witnesses.

The disciples *didn't* give their lives while He was alive, but they *did* give their lives after He died and rose. This is unquestionable proof that the resurrection, and the promise of the Father being given, is the premise of God's intended Christianity. *That is…* to be bold!

Fortunately for us, this miraculous and promised occurrence for the Jewish believers was only the beginning of God's plan. He purposed for *all* who would call upon His name to be saved, filled by His Spirit, and empowered to be His witnesses.

With that said, let us now discuss the correlation between Solomon's

Temple being filled with God's glory and the Holy Spirit filling the disciples at Pentecost.

The Promise Of The Father

There are two accounts in the Old Testament that parallel our walk today in light of our redemption. Firstly, the Lord saving us, and secondly, being filled with the Holy Spirit. These accounts, without coincidence, are both found within the life of Solomon. In the first chapter of 2nd Chronicles, the typology of being born-again is revealed:

> *"In that night did God appear unto Solomon, and said unto him, Ask what I shall give thee. And Solomon said unto God, Thou hast shewed great mercy unto David my father, and hast made me to reign in his stead. Now, O Lord God, let thy promise unto David my father be established..." (2nd Chronicles 1:7-9) (emphasis mine)*

The promise of the Father, of course, is the Holy Spirit:

> *"And, being assembled together with them, commanded them that they should not depart from Jerusalem, but wait for the promise of the Father, which, saith he, ye have heard of me. For John truly baptized with water; but ye shall be baptized with the Holy Ghost not many days hence." (Acts 1:4, 5) (emphasis mine)*

Now, you may be thinking, "Wasn't the promise of the Father for the disciples, the baptism in the Holy Spirit... not being born again? Weren't they born-again when Jesus breathed on them?" Yes! The disciples received the Holy Spirit before the day of Pentecost, just like Solomon received wisdom before the glory of the Lord filled the temple.

> *"And when he had said this, he breathed on them [His Disciples], and saith unto them, Receive ye the Holy Ghost." (John 20:22) (brackets mine)*

The disciples had new life breathed into them at this moment by the Last Adam, like the first Adam did in the garden. A brand-new start! This was the born-again experience for the disciples. Due to Jesus' finished work and resurrection, they were regenerated by the Holy Spirit. Shortly after this occurrence, the Lord Jesus told His disciples to wait in the upper room for the promise of the Father. This was separate from their initial encounter with the resurrected Christ after He breathed on them.

Solomon asking for the promise of his father, David, to be established was a prophetic declaration towards the Christ to come. As explained in the previous chapter, Jesus was the promised King that would never cease from sitting on David's throne (Jeremiah 33:17). Though Solomon was asking for his current kingdom to be governed with wisdom and knowledge from on high, unbeknownst to him, he was asking what we *all* ask today in regard to salvation; that is, for Jesus to sit upon the throne of our hearts and to reign through us with His wisdom and might.

> *"But of him are ye in* ***Christ Jesus, who of God is made unto us wisdom****, and righteousness, and sanctification, and redemption." (1st Corinthians 1:30) (emphasis mine)*

> ***"Give me now wisdom*** *and knowledge, that I may go out and come in before this people: for who can judge this thy people, that is so great? And God said to Solomon, Because this was in thine heart, and thou hast not asked riches, wealth, or honour, nor the life of thine enemies, neither yet hast asked long life; but hast asked wisdom and knowledge for thyself, that thou mayest judge my people, over whom I have made thee king: Wisdom and knowledge is granted unto thee; and I will give thee riches, and wealth, and honour, such as none of the kings have had that have been before thee, neither shall there any after thee have the like." (2nd Chronicles 1:10-12) (emphasis mine)*

Solomon received all that He would ever need to successfully reign in this encounter. The wisdom Solomon gained from this impartation caused his kingdom's reach to surpass that of his father, David.

Now, Solomon could have had all the resources that his father provided… which he did… he could have had the blueprint, the people, and the territory… which he did… but he wouldn't have had the ability to implement the plan without the wisdom *and* power.

For many Christians, they have everything they will ever need invested within them at salvation, yet they are either ignorant to the baptism of the Holy Spirit, or worse yet, they are filled but are still living for themselves. Regardless, both cases will completely undermine the Lord's intent for them to be His witnesses.

This was brought to light to clear up some common misconceptions about salvation and the baptism of the Holy Spirit. When we receive Jesus and become born again, we *do* receive the Holy Spirit. It is not as if we receive Jesus at salvation and the Holy Spirit when baptized. Nor is it that we receive some of the Holy Spirit at salvation and the rest of Him upon His baptism. We receive *all* of the Lord upon salvation. In fact, we receive all of the Father at salvation! However, the baptism of the Holy Spirit is permitting Him to take over *all* of us. We will soon discuss what it means to be His witnesses.

Firstly, let's consider a few verses here to justify how sure our salvation is, yet at the same time, prove the case for the necessary baptism in the Holy Spirit.

> *In whom ye also trusted, after that ye heard the word of truth, the gospel of your salvation: in whom also after that ye believed, ye were sealed with that holy Spirit of promise." (Ephesians 1:13)*

Here in Ephesians, we are told that after we believe, we are sealed with the Holy Spirit. This refers to our born-again, righteous spirit being sealed with the Holy Spirit upon our faith and trust in the finished works of Jesus. This refers to being born-again yet receiving the Holy Spirit at the same time. Even so, this is the initial regeneration.

Some Christians mistakenly believe it is unnecessary to be baptized in the Holy Spirit and assume that regeneration is the only step needed. While others are confused because they believe they are not saved unless they speak in tongues. In my biblical opinion, neither are true. It is necessary to be baptized in the Holy Spirit after being regenerated (born-again), and you can be saved without speaking in tongues.

I'm sure I don't need to do much convincing here in regard to the Trinity and Them being One, but I would like to highlight a few passages in hopes of clarifying *Who* we get at salvation.

> *Even the* ***Spirit of truth****; whom the world cannot receive, because it*

> *seeth him not, neither knoweth him: but ye know him;* ***for he dwelleth with you, and shall be in you.*** *(John 14:17)*

"For he dwelleth with you", this is referring to Jesus. He was dwelling *with* the disciples. "*And shall be in you.*" He would then dwell *within* them!

Jesus is the Spirit of Truth… and so is the Holy Spirit! Just in case you're unsure of this, Jesus said in the very next verse how *He* would come to them:

> *"I will not leave you comfortless: I will come to you." (John 14:18)*

Consider this verse:

> *"And because ye are sons, God hath sent forth the* ***Spirit of his Son*** *into your hearts, crying, Abba, Father." (Galatians 4:6)*

How awesome!

Now, there are more verses that give interchangeable titles to the Lord, such as Jesus being the Everlasting Father, as mentioned in Isaiah, and the Holy Spirit being the Teacher. But this next verse really seals the deal on our God being three in One.

> *"For in him [Christ] dwelleth all the fulness of the Godhead bodily." (Colossians 2:9) (brackets mine)*

Being that the Godhead dwells fully in Christ, and by being born-again, we receive Jesus, we, therefore, receive the Father and the Holy Spirit upon regeneration. This is not to say they are not distinct, but only to say they are One. Hopefully, this clears up any confusion if you don't speak in tongues and are wondering if you are truly saved or not. Speaking in tongues does not save you… it is the confession from your tongue that Jesus Christ is Lord that does. If you have been undeniably changed from the faith of the gospel being preached, conceived, and birthed in your heart… if you have surrendered your life to Him and have wholeheartedly accepted Him as Lord… yet you do not speak in tongues: rest assured, you are saved. Nevertheless, there is more for you!

Consuming Fire

> *"Now when Solomon had made an end of praying, the fire came down*

from heaven, and consumed the burnt offering and the sacrifices; and the glory of the LORD filled the house." (2nd Chronicles 7:1)

Consider this comforting passage… we are the burnt offering!

"I beseech you therefore, brethren, by the mercies of God, that ye present your bodies a living sacrifice, holy, acceptable unto God, which is your reasonable service." (Romans 12:1)

Rest assured, all that's being consumed is who you aren't. All to reveal the new man. One who would walk according to the Spirit and not according to the flesh. A burnt offering for His glory. This is the price that Jesus paid for you. To be one with Him.

Solomon built a house for the glory of the Lord, and as discussed in the previous chapter, you are the house Jesus built for the Lord's glory—a temple for Him to call home.

"Then said Solomon, The LORD hath said that he would dwell in the thick darkness. But I have built an house of habitation for thee, and a place for thy dwelling for ever." (2nd Chronicles 6:1-2)

Then, Solomon prayed for the temple that would be filled with His glory in 2nd Chronicles chapter 6, and in the 7th chapter the Lord answered.

"…the fire came down from heaven, and consumed the burnt offering and the sacrifices; and the glory of the LORD filled the house. And the priests could not enter into the house of the LORD, because the glory of the LORD had filled the LORD's house." (2nd Chronicles 7:1-2)

Jesus prayed for the temple that would be filled with His glory as well!

"These words spake Jesus, and lifted up his eyes to heaven, and said, Father, the hour is come; glorify thy Son, that thy Son also may glorify thee…I have glorified thee on the earth: I have finished the work which thou gavest me to do…I have manifested thy name unto the men which thou gavest me out of the world: thine they were, and thou gavest them me; and they have kept thy word…I pray for them: I pray not for the world, but for them which thou hast given me; for they are thine…Neither pray I for these alone, but for them also which shall

> *believe on me through their word; That they all may be one; as thou, Father, art in me, and I in thee, that they also may be one in us: that the world may believe that thou hast sent me." (John 17:1, 4, 6, 9, 20-21)*

Something wonderful to consider is how the first to pray for your salvation was Jesus Himself!

> *"Neither pray I for these alone, but for them also which shall believe on me through their word." (John 17:20)*

Jesus prayed for you to be saved! Hallelujah!

Now, being that Solomon's enlightened construction of the temple foreshadows Christ, the builder, and how the temple being filled with the Lord's glory speaks of the baptism of the Holy Spirit, let us now focus all our attention on the reason Solomon's account was written in the first place.

You Shall Be My Witnesses

> *"But ye shall receive power, after that the Holy Ghost is come upon you: and ye shall be witnesses unto me both in Jerusalem, and in all Judaea, and in Samaria, and unto the uttermost part of the earth." (Acts 1:8)*

Jesus said that we would become His witnesses. The word *witness*, or *martus* in Greek, stems from the word *martyr*. A martyr is one who refuses to deny their beliefs and chooses death instead. Though it is possible… *and in the days to come likely*… to lose your life for the gospel's sake, don't worry… we are called to lose our lives from the start! Being baptized with the Holy Spirit, and becoming Jesus' witnesses, is synonymous with being put to death. How so? Allow me to explain:

> *"And for this cause he is the mediator of the new testament, that by means of death, for the redemption of the transgressions that were under the first testament, they which are called might receive the promise of eternal inheritance. For where a testament is, there must also of necessity be the death of the testator. For a testament is of force after men are dead: otherwise it is of no strength at all while the*

testator liveth." (Hebrews 9:15-17)

This passage found in Hebrews is extremely revelatory in regard to His will being effective in our lives. It takes death in order for a will to be inherited. If your grandfather has you named in his will to receive a gift upon his passing, it requires just that: for him to pass! Otherwise, it is still in his possession while he lives.

"For where a testament is, there must also of necessity be the death of the testator." (Hebrews 9:16)

What this passage in Hebrews is saying, is that for a will to be given over, the testator, or the will maker, must pass away. This is what Jesus did. He died in order to create a New Testament. However, there is a contingency found in the following verse that applies to us. Jesus finished His part, but we have a part to play:

"For a testament is of force after men are dead: otherwise it is of no strength at all while the testator liveth." (Hebrews 9:17)

The New Testament is of force *after* men are dead! Jesus died for us to receive the greatest inheritance of all. It's called the gospel! However, in order for the gospel to be effectively witnessed by the world through us, it takes our death as well. This is actually in bold letters in the will, not fine print:

"For if ye live after the flesh, ye shall die: but if ye through the Spirit do mortify the deeds of the body, ye shall live. For as many as are led by the Spirit of God, they are the sons of God." (Romans 8:13-14)

"I beseech you therefore, brethren, by the mercies of God, that ye present your bodies a living sacrifice, holy, acceptable unto God, which is your reasonable service." (Romans 12:1)

"I am crucified with Christ: nevertheless I live; yet not I, but Christ liveth in me: and the life which I now live in the flesh I live by the faith of the Son of God, who loved me, and gave himself for me." (Galatians 2:20)

Now, in order for the Holy Spirit to have His way with us as He did with Jesus, we must lay our lives down well before we are ever faced with possible martyrdom. Jesus was a martyr long before He laid His physical life down at Calvary. Fortunately, Jesus made it simple enough for us to follow Him. We must go ahead and die already:

> *"Then said Jesus unto his disciples, If any man will come after me, let him deny himself, and take up his cross, and follow me." (Matthew 16:24)*

Picking up our cross then becomes the prerequisite for the Holy Spirit's takeover. When it comes to being led by the Spirit, the cross becomes as the sail to our ship.

> *"The wind bloweth where it listeth [chooses, pleases], and thou hearest the sound thereof, but canst not tell whence it cometh, and whither it goeth: so is every one that is born of the Spirit." (John 3:8) (brackets mine)*

Wind And Fire

> *"...he shall baptize you with the Holy Ghost, and with fire." (Matthew 3:11)*

On the day of Pentecost, an extremely significant thing transpired. Remember Babel and how each man set their mind to build a tower to heaven? At that time, they were all of one language. The Lord Himself came down and confounded their work because they were unified for evil. This goes to prove how powerful unity is! Even though it was for the wrong, the Lord said nothing would restrain them in what they imagined doing (Genesis 11:6). Therefore, *He* stopped it.

The Lord scattered them across the earth with different languages. They could no longer understand each other nor build together in unity. This was *His* doing. These men tried to build a means to heaven in their own strength. See, it wasn't about men building their way up but about God coming down. Jesus made the way for man! Not through a tower but through the cross. The cross bridged the gap, and the Lord did it Himself... as a man. Hallelujah!

Without coincidence, the disciples began to speak in tongues and drew all from afar as the Holy Spirit descended at Pentecost. At Babel, all were confounded and given different languages, but at Pentecost, the Holy Spirit drew them back!

> *"Now when this was noised abroad, the multitude came together, and were* ***confounded****, because that every man heard them speak in his own language. And they were all amazed and marvelled, saying one to another, Behold, are not all these which speak Galilaeans? And how hear we every man in our own tongue, wherein we were born? Parthians, and Medes, and Elamites, and the dwellers in Mesopotamia, and in Judaea, and Cappadocia, in Pontus, and Asia, Phrygia, and Pamphylia, in Egypt, and in the parts of Libya about Cyrene, and strangers of Rome, Jews and proselytes, Cretes and Arabians, we do hear them speak in our tongues the wonderful works of God." (Acts 2:6-11) (emphasis mine)*

The word confounded was used both in Genesis when discussing the tower of Babel and in the book of Acts when discussing the day of Pentecost. This is certainly without coincidence. The Holy Spirit unified these men around the finished works of Jesus, not around a man-made plan to eternal life. There are plenty of "religions" out there that are unified for the wrong cause. Unfortunately, they are centered around a counterfeit means to heaven. Now, *after* Jesus made the way, and through the power of the Holy Spirit, we can work together in unity, declaring the way He paved.

Jesus said He would build His church upon the revelation of Him as Christ and that the gates of hell would not prevail against it (Matthew 16:18). Hell might encourage slime and brick to be built in place of stone and mortar, but it will certainly not encourage the declaration of the gospel of Jesus Christ, which is the true and only way (John 14:6). Therefore, the devil comes to now confound the way Jesus paved through disunity! The word *confound* means *"to throw into disorder."* We must not be ignorant of his devices and endeavor to keep the unity of the Spirit as it declares in Ephesians.

God threw in disorder the building plans of Babel and caused them to separate, but later, The Holy Spirit threw in disorder the ones who were separated to unify them once more!

Godly unity is so powerful that the Lord Himself commanded a blessing upon it, as found in Psalm 133. This is one of only two places where a blessing is *commanded* by the Lord!

> *"Behold, how good and how pleasant it is for brethren to dwell together in unity...for there the LORD commanded the blessing, even life for evermore." (Psalm 133:1, 3)*

Though the devil seeks to steal, kill, and destroy, and though he desires nothing more than to disrupt the Lord's building plans... he will never prevail against His church.

Now, regarding the unity the Lord brought together at Pentecost, consider how the Holy Spirit came. There was a sound as of a mighty rushing wind, and there appeared cloven tongues like fire above the people's heads (Acts 2:1-3). This is remarkable when taking into consideration what originally transpired at Babel. At Babel, the men's tongues were changed, and their speech was indistinguishable, whereas, on the day of Pentecost, the disciples' tongues were changed by the power of the Holy Spirit and clearly recognized. What were they doing? They were declaring the *works of God* in each language... not the *works of men* who tried to build at Babel!

Furthermore, consider how wind and fire don't mix well. If you were to have a fire start in the woods without wind, you would gain more time to put it out. However, if it were to be windy along with the fire, it would be nearly impossible to contain. You would have to simply wait for nature to take its course. This is what I believe is being portrayed regarding the Holy Spirit's infilling at Pentecost. He desires for our tongues to be set ablaze with the word of the gospel and for His wind and leading to take us wherever He desires. The result of this mixture would be utter devastation to the enemy's camp!

Consider how in the early church, the cities would experience revival when the disciples would go and preach. They couldn't be contained! The envious rulers sought to mitigate the preaching through imprisonment, beatings, and death, but persecution only caused the fire to gain more ground as the disciples were scattered. Initially, the men of Babel were scattered abroad, not understanding each other, but now the disciples were scattered with fiery tongues bringing those back on track! Not to continue building around a self-centered plan… but now according to God's Christ-centered plan. His plan is not confusing or complicated. It is precise and clear. There is one way to heaven, and His name is Jesus Christ!

> *"This is the LORD'S doing; it is marvellous in our eyes." (Psalm 118:23)*

Now, in conclusion, it is imperative to touch on what we briefly spoke about in this chapter's introduction. That is, our well being filled with the earth.

The Ear and Eye Gate

> *"The heart is deceitful above all things, and desperately wicked: who can know it?" (Jeremiah 17:9)*

There is a great hinderance to the work of the Holy Spirit within a believer's life. It is doubt and unbelief. Now, Jesus said that it wasn't what went into a man that defiled him, but what came out of him. Which, if I may preface, is obviously true:

> *"Not that which goeth into the mouth defileth a man; but that which cometh out of the mouth, this defileth a man." (Matthew 15:11)*

However, notice how it says it's not what goes into the *mouth* that defiles a man. That which goes into the mouth is physical, yet that which goes into the *ear* is spiritual. Interestingly, it's called an ear *canal*. A canal is a passageway!

This also confirms how the heart is immeasurably more precious than the stomach. Jesus goes on to explain how that which goes into the mouth comes out as waste, whereas that which comes out of the heart is the real issue at hand. The Pharisees were watching what they ate and were washing their hands often in hopes of keeping their temples clean. Jesus explained how man's heart was the source of defilement, not dirty hands, of course.

Jesus then goes on to explain what He was referring to:

> *"O generation of vipers, how can ye, being evil, speak good things? for out of the abundance of the heart the mouth speaketh. A good man*

out of the good treasure of the heart bringeth forth good things: and an evil man out of the evil treasure bringeth forth evil things." (Matthew 12:34-35)

Jesus' words bring us a lot of clarity. What Jesus said in the gospel's regarding a good and an evil man bringing forth treasure is what was *already* there. "For out of the abundance, *or overflow*, of the heart, the mouth speaks" (Luke 6:45). What is already there comes out! It is either a polluted well or a clean one. The choice is what we allow *in* now as believers, not by way of the mouth (which is what Jesus was referring to when rebuking the Pharisees), but by way of the entrances into our soul.

This is why Jesus boldly confronted the hypocrisy of the Pharisees and the Sadducees. They thought that by watching the food they ate, washing their hands, and "keeping" the Law, that they were clean. This was their great deception. They were defiled from the start! Not only the Pharisees for that matter, but all. All those without Christ need a new well. The righteous in the Old Testament were righteous by faith, not by their works. Our righteousness is as filthy rags apart from Christ's righteousness imparted unto us. Do you know what filthy rags are? They are used menstrual cloths. It is blood that cannot produce life.

Those who *do* have Christ have *become* undefiled, not by what came out of their heart, but by Who came in! We no longer have a desperately wicked heart but a brand new one that ever desires the things of the Lord. The tree and the ground have become good! Now, we must keep it.

"A new heart also will I give you, and a new spirit will I put within you: and I will take away the stony heart out of your flesh, and I will give you an heart of flesh." (Ezekiel 36:26)

It is important to understand the context in what Jesus was saying to the Pharisees in regard to that which comes out of the heart in defiling a man. Some believers think they still have a sinful nature or a wicked heart. In reality, it's not a wicked heart but the residue from their unrenewed mind that must be washed by the water of His Word.

Though Jesus said it wasn't what went into a man that defiled him, but what came out of his heart, in context, we find this due to the fact that the

Pharisees needed open heart surgery before they changed their diet. Being that we allowed the Great Physician to remove our old hearts altogether, we *now* must consider our diet. What comes out of our heart is what now goes into our heart through the eye and ear gates. Watching what goes into the soulish part of our hearts via the eye or the ear gate is of utmost importance for the believer because it will either hinder or enable the Holy Spirit's flow.

With that said, the scripture says that the Holy Spirit would bring the words of Jesus to our remembrance. Scripture must then be continuously put before our eyes and ears so the Holy Spirit has something to work with! This is where biblical meditation comes in.

> *"But the Comforter, which is the Holy Ghost, whom the Father will send in my name, he shall teach you all things, and bring all things to your remembrance, whatsoever I have said unto you." (John 14:26)*

I once had a vision of Jesus in the garden of my heart with His hands out, and He said to me, *"Give me seeds."* Our co-laboring with Him will enable His working within. The seed of God's Word does the work. It accomplishes what it was sent forth to do. With that said, what happens when the seeds of God's Word aren't being sown, but contradicting worldly seeds are? They also accomplish what they are sent forth to do! They bind His holy hands from the good work within. Not to say that He has thorny vines wrapped around His arms, but that He is limited in what He desires to do because we are neglecting our part. In turn, we are co-laboring with the devil and are allowing our well and garden to be dammed up and hedged in.

If Jesus wants His seed to be sown, which is His Word, so does the enemy want his seed to be sown, which is that of this world. For this cause, we must guard our hearts with all diligence and be filled with the Word of God. In turn, the Holy Spirit can then flow through us without obstruction.

> *"For if the firstfruit be holy, the lump is also holy: and if the root be holy, so are the branches." (Romans 11:16)*

See, the lump is holy. This is why Jesus said to beware of the leaven! There are many factors involved when considering walking in faith. We truly have all the faith we need because we live by the faith of the Son of God, yet we often are so encumbered by doubt that we negate it.

For instance, the scripture says, "God calls those things that are not as if they were" (Romans 4:17). Yet, if we are allowing our eyes to dictate what is, instead of what the word says truly is, we can never call those things that we are seeing to be removed because we have dammed up the river's flow. On the other hand, if we are hearing "God calls those things that are not as if they were" *more* than what we are seeing, we can operate in unobstructed faith. Your physical eyes will either be subject to the eyes of your heart or the ways of the world. The choice is determined by the concentration of either the word or the world. It doesn't take much dirt to contaminate water. However, it doesn't take much faith to remove a mountain!

The labor for a believer is found in choosing to read God's Word. It is not so much of a labor to sit and watch a movie, but it is to come against the immature areas of our souls and to get into the Bible. When we choose to be disciplined in the Word of God, we then train our senses (Hebrews 5:14). Apart from receiving the Word of God daily, the life-giving well within will be stopped up with dirt, and the canals of our soul will be contaminated. We will desire to see the mountain removed, but our eyes will be considering the situation rather than the surety of His promises. How could we then call those things that aren't as though they are if *facts* take preeminence? We cannot. Though something can be a fact according to the world's standards, it doesn't mean it is truth according to the kingdom of God.

From the next chapter on, we will be discussing what transpires within our soul when confronted with the Word of God. Meditating on God's Word will cause His enemies to scatter. Surprisingly, His enemies today are not without but within. The unrenewed mind is the enemy of God.

6

Ziklag

"And it came to pass, when David and his men were come to Ziklag on the third day, that the Amalekites had invaded the south, and Ziklag, and smitten Ziklag, and burned it with fire." (1st Samuel 30:1)

There is a facet of God's glory buried in the Philistine town of Ziklag that is well worth unearthing. If you haven't guessed by now, Jesus is the treasure. This chapter will be devoted to what He singlehandedly recovered for us at redemption. The tool we will use to uncover Christ will be the emotionally taxing yet greatly rewarding "Ziklag" season for David.

What Jesus recovered for us at Calvary or Golgotha has been greatly misunderstood by most throughout the body of Christ. Many believe Jesus paid the price for us to get to heaven, when in fact, He paid the price to get heaven into us.

"Neither shall they say, Lo here! or, lo there! for, behold, ***the kingdom of God is within you.****" (Luke 17:21) (emphasis mine)*

Calvary is transliterated from the Latin word *calvaria*, meaning "*the skull of an animal or human.*" It is the same meaning as the Greek word *kranion*, where we get the word *cranium* in English. Without coincidence, Jesus crushed the skull of the serpent on Calvary's hill and recovered that which was lost in the Garden. The authority is held in the head. Jesus became the Head of His body through what transpired at Calvary!

"And I will put enmity between thee and the woman, and between thy seed and her seed; it shall bruise thy head, and thou shalt bruise his heel." (Genesis 3:15)

This prophecy was to the seed of the woman, which was Christ, in regard to Jesus' crucifixion. At Calvary, Jesus defeated the enemy through death by crushing his head, but Jesus' heel was bruised in the process (His death). Jesus died righteous, even as a man would stand tall in stepping on a snake. Jesus was not crushed through death. The devil was. Though Jesus was bruised through death in the process of destroying the devil, He could not be held by it.

When it comes to the Garden, Adam wandered far from its perfection when cast away from it. With each step he took away from Eden, his recollection of it faded. At his death, he couldn't have been farther from the Garden. Therefore, the Last Adam came to show us the way back.

This chapter will be dedicated to using biblical examples to show how Jesus renews our minds today. Like the Children of Israel traveled *back* to paradise (being that Abraham was in the promised land initially), so are we on a journey back to where it all began.

Moreover, Saul, David, and Solomon's kingdoms will be compared to our walk today with the Lord. The Bible has a recurring theme of salvation buried in the Old Testament, and the reign of these three kings correlate perfectly. Saul represents the flesh, David represents the soul, and Solomon represents the Spirit. Jesus conquered death in the flesh, He conquers our unrenewed mind with His Word, and He reigns supreme in our spirit. When our soul aligns with our spirit, our whole body becomes the kingdom fit for the King.

Lastly, David recovering all of what the Amalekites had stolen from him in Ziklag will paint the most beautiful picture of what Jesus recovered for us at redemption. *Jesus recovered all.*

Pressed Down/Poured Out

The Biblical name meaning of Ziklag has uncertain roots. A few sources claim it derives from two ancient Hebrew words coming together to mean "*to press*" and "*to pour.*" Another source similarly claims the meaning to be "*measure pressed down.*" The Strong's Concordance does not supply Ziklag's etymology, but the Blue Letter Bible defines it as "*winding.*" Though the name itself does not have a definitive meaning, David's history with Ziklag is certain: he was pressed down, he was poured out, and he came out victorious.

After tirelessly circumventing Saul throughout most of Israel, David sought refuge in the enemy-occupied area of Philistia. He entered the land hoping to discourage Saul from further pursuing him and his men. This bold plan worked, and according to 1st Samuel 27:4, Saul relented after hearing David had fled to Gath.

While in Gath, David found favor with Achish, the Philistine king, and Ziklag was given to him and his men to occupy. David lived in the Philistine's territory for nearly a year and a half. He and his men would raid enemy-occupied towns but make the king believe he was attacking his own people. When asked by the king what he had done that day, he answered by saying, *"We raided through the south of Judah..."* (1st Samuel 27:10). When they attacked a city, they left no one alive in the area they destroyed to say otherwise! Achish believed David, and said, *"Surely, he has made his own people to loathe him! He shall be my servant forever"* (1st Samuel 27:12).

On a certain day following, the Philistine army gathered to fight against Israel. David is summoned by Achish and is told that he and his men will also be joining forces! David (truly playing the part here) assures Achish that he and his men will prove their loyalty toward him. Achish is ever more impressed by his newfound captain.

Now, we know from already reading the account that David was prohibited from partnering with Philistia… but we are left to imagine what was going on in David's mind leading up to it! He was marching towards his own people for war! Those of you who are like me are left with these unanswered questions: *"Would David have fought against his own people if the princes didn't stop him? Would he and his men have skipped out on the fight altogether? Were they somehow in communications with others in Israel explaining the plan?"* We simply do not know.

After the Philistine princes saw David and his men prepared for battle, they rebuked Achish for his trust in him. They said, *"What better time for David to reconcile with Saul then to turn on us in battle and deliver us into his hand?"* From the perspective of these Philistine princes, it was wise to assume the worst in what David and his men could have done. After this, David and his men were forced to retreat.

On a side note, I don't believe *everything* that happens is God's will. In my opinion, some take the sovereignty of God to a place that contradicts scripture! Consider this: was it God's will to stop David from battling his own people, but not God's will to stop him from killing Uriah? Was it God's will for Saul to be raised as king, only to be replaced by David? God Himself said that Saul's kingdom would have been established forever if he had obeyed him! Yet he sinned, and his kingdom was removed.

On the other hand, David sinned, yet his kingdom was established! Where is the line drawn concerning God's sovereign will and intervention and man's will? Now, to stay on track, I cannot delve deep into this topic, but I highly recommend reading Andrew Wommack's book *"The True Nature of God"* for the best take on God's sovereignty you'll most likely ever hear.

All things considered, there is no way to guarantee what would have ultimately happened if David had been forced to fight. We are left with our own presumptions. For what it's worth, I believe the Lord intervened among the princes and caused David and his men to retreat to Ziklag. Moreover, if all went according to Achish's initial request, I do not believe David would have fought against his own people.

Finally, David returns to a burning Ziklag. Afterward, he encourages himself in the Lord to pursue and overtake the enemy, which stole everything away, concluding this dramatic timeframe of David's life. Though Ziklag was a winding road according to its own name, the recovery of David and his men's possessions will be our final destination. Undoubtedly, Jesus will be observed in David's repossessing victory.

Gethsemane

> *"And it came to pass, when David and his men were come to Ziklag on* ***the third day****, that the Amalekites had invaded the south, and Ziklag, and smitten Ziklag, and burned it with fire." (1st Samuel 30:1) (emphasis mine)*

What's notable from the passage mentioned above is how David and his men returned to Ziklag on the *third day*, and all their possessions and families were stolen. Though tragic and seemingly hopeless, the third day is mentioned yet again in foreshadowing the Christ to come. If I were to do a word study on the number "three" or the "third day," I could safely bet that David's life story would mention it the most. Yet there is a third-day story that tops them all. Regarding Jesus and His resurrection, He recovered *all* that the enemy had stolen… which was *us*!

Before discussing what David recovered and how it foreshadows Jesus, let's first consider the unthinkable scene for him and his men upon their return to Ziklag. Now, *we would certainly assume* that David and his company were relieved in retreating from civil war… nevertheless, their consolation would be short lived. Their emotions would soon be overloaded. Thus the "windings" of Ziklag are proven. Upon arrival, David and his men are consumed with despair when discovering their homes and families were bereaved, and their city was altogether burned to the ground. All was stolen from them. All the men could do was weep:

> *"So David and his men came to the city, and, behold, it was burned with fire; and their wives, and their sons, and their daughters, were taken captives.* ***Then David*** *and the people that were with him lifted up their voice and* ***wept****, until they had no more power to weep." (1st Samuel 30:3-4) (emphasis mine)*

Due to only looking for Jesus while studying scripture, I couldn't help but notice Him within these two verses mentioned above. However, the sixth verse more appropriately serves the purpose of our discussion. Consider this:

> *"****And David was greatly distressed****; for the people spake of stoning him, because the soul of all the people was grieved, every man for his sons and for his daughters:* ***but David encouraged himself in the LORD his God****." (1st Samuel 30:6) (emphasis mine)*

Take note of how David and his men were all affected by the same situation, yet David wound up becoming the scapegoat. Though he was faultless in the matter, David was facing being put to death for what the enemy had stolen! Nevertheless, David stood alone and encouraged himself in the Lord. All things considered, only one scapegoat was *completely* innocent in the matter. Though David was facing great persecution from his own people, it pales in comparison to the relentless persecution and crucifixion of Christ.

"And David's two wives were taken captives…" (1st Samuel 30:5)

Keep in mind how the scripture states that David's wives were taken captive.

Now…consider Jesus!

This is precisely what transpired with Jesus in Gethsemane. Remember when Jesus asked Peter, *"Could you not pray with me for one hour?"* Jesus was left alone!

> *"And David was greatly distressed…" (1st Samuel 30:6)*

Like David felt the weight of blame placed upon his shoulders, so much more did Jesus experience an unfathomable transfer of fault in Gethsemane. Jesus earnestly prayed in "great distress" like David did in Ziklag. Both encouraged themselves in the Lord! Unlike David, however, Jesus was about to take the sin of the world upon Himself.

> *"…for the people spake of stoning him, because the soul of all the people was grieved…" (1st Samuel 30:6)*

In further comparison, David's physical life was in jeopardy due to what the enemy had stolen. He was facing death by his own men. Jesus' own Jewish brothers (at that time while in Gethsemane) were also plotting His death. Like David found himself alone to encourage himself in the Lord while his own plotted to kill him, so did Jesus find Himself alone in effectual prayer to His Father concerning His impending death as well.

Moreover, Jesus faced death for what the enemy had stolen… his bride! He rescued His bride!

Imagine how triumphant David must have become in the eyes of his wives after they were saved. Picture one of those climactic movie scenes where the damsel in distress is impossibly rescued. What unspeakable gratitude emerges from the actress! Now picture David and his men really doing it! Truth be told, the book is always better than the movie anyway. With this in mind, how *much more* can we now highly esteem the One who delivered us from hell and death?

Now, if this didn't parallel the passion of Christ enough for you, perhaps this connection will: Did you know what the name *Gethsemane* means in

Hebrew? Similar to Ziklag's etymology, Gethsemane derives from two Hebrew words: *"gat,"* meaning *"a place for pressing oils (or wines),"* and *shemanim*, which means *"oils."* Without coincidence, *Ziklag* means *"to press"* and *"to pour,"* and *Gethsemane* means *"olive oil press."* They are both a place of pressing. However, David's pressing (though real) was only a type and a shadow of the pressing of Christ. For that matter, David couldn't offer his men or us what Jesus could and did. Jesus was *literally* crushed and pressed for us and ultimately killed. From His pressing and crushing alone came our redemption.

Finally, when David fled to Philistia, hoping to dismay Saul, he met Achish in Gath. *"Gath"* uncoincidentally means *"winepress."* One of the things I believe the Lord would have us glean from this account is what olives and grapes produce. Olives, of course, produce olive oil, and grapes produce wine. In context, Jesus came to a place where He was crushed and poured out for us. From Him alone came the oil and the wine.

> *"I have trodden the winepress alone; and of the people there was none with me..." (Isaiah 63:3)*

Sidetrack with me for a moment to discuss a parable that is too close in comparison to avoid. Oil and wine are specifically mentioned, and Jesus is evidently seen.

The Good Samaritan

> *"And, behold, a certain lawyer stood up, and tempted him, saying, Master, what shall I do to* ***inherit eternal life?****...But he, willing to justify himself, said unto Jesus, And who is my neighbour? And Jesus answering said, A certain man went down from Jerusalem to Jericho, and fell among thieves,* ***which stripped him of his raiment, and wounded him, and departed, leaving him half dead****...But a certain Samaritan, as he journeyed, came where he was: and when he saw him, he had compassion on him, And went to him, and bound up his wounds,* ***pouring in oil and wine****, and set him on his own beast, and brought him to an inn, and took care of him." (Luke 10:25, 29-30, 33-34) (emphasis mine)*

Remember the parable of the "good" Samaritan? Remember the position the "certain man" was left in? Interestingly, the "certain man" in this story was beaten, robbed, stripped of his clothing, and left alone to die.

Allow me to propose a more than likely theory—one in which I am completely convinced of. Perhaps I can persuade you as well. I believe the "Good Samaritan" and the "certain man" are one in the same. I believe this story highlights two aspects of the place Jesus *took* for us (the certain man) and the place Jesus *gave* to us (the Good Samaritan).

Who was betrayed by a thief (Judas), stripped and robbed of His clothing (Roman soldiers), and beaten by the same until He was nearly killed? Need I answer?

This "certain man" was wounded, clothe-less, and lay dying on the roadside. He was carelessly passed over by his own countrymen. *Jesus,* while hanging naked on the cross, and after being beaten and marred more than any man in history, is gazed upon boldly by His people shaking their heads in shame (Isaiah 52:14, Psalm 22:7, Matthew 27:39). He too was passed over.

Additionally, this "certain man" took our place. That was us wallowing in sin and shame, beaten on the side of the road! Correspondingly, we also fit the mold of this certain man. Whether we realized it or not, we were stripped of our clothing (righteousness), robbed by an enemy (the devil), and left half dead. All those without Christ are walking around half dead (physically alive but spiritually dead), stripped of their identity and crushed by sin! We were all together in such a case!

But God!

Next thing we know, a *"Good Samaritan"* comes our way (A *stranger* if you would.) and pours in oil and wine to bind up our wounds. Through sin, we were so far removed from God and His ways that we naturally became His enemy. Nevertheless, the Lord had such compassion upon us, like the good Samaritan did towards the certain man, that while we were yet sinners, Christ died for us (Romans 5:8). God was not our Father, nor Jesus our Neighbor, when He gave His Life for us over 2000 years ago… we were strangers and enemies! Yet this "Stranger" became our neighbor and is a friend that sticks closer than a brother today.

Not by chance, the Jews and the Samaritans were also opposed to one another. They were not friendly neighbors! This is one reason I believe Jesus used this parable when addressing the lawyer's initial question about inheriting eternal life. Mankind was naturally opposed to God, and to inherit eternal life would require peace from a war that only God Himself could settle. The Prince of Peace *made* peace through His cross.

> *"And, having made peace through the blood of his cross, by him to reconcile all things unto himself; by him, I say, whether they be things in earth, or things in heaven." (Colossians 1:20)*

In addition, when comparing this story to Jesus, it becomes evident that none of the Jews who passed by the certain man could truly help... *even if they wanted to*! No priest nor Levite raised up in the law could redeem the state of fallen man. It would take an outsider.

Did you know that Samaritans are half Jew and half Gentile? This, yet again, portrays Jesus in regard to this parable. Though Jesus was not half man and half God, nor half Jew and half Gentile for that matter... He was the best of both worlds: wholly God and wholly man. The outsider sent to pour in the oil and wine into the stranger's wounds.

Hallelujah!

Regarding what we recently discussed concerning the pressings of Gethsemane and the fate of His crucifixion... Jesus alone produced the oil and the wine! Jesus Himself was the cure! The wine is His blood, and the oil is His Spirit. This was the only cure for the fallen state of man. The Great Physician had the cure in His blood. He was the Doctor and the Donor. He was the Priest and the Offering.

What Jesus faced in having our iniquities placed upon Himself (Isaiah 53:6) and being separated from His Father because of it (Isaiah 54:7) can never be fathomed on this side of heaven. The crushing weight of sin upon His shoulders was much heavier than the cross itself. Only He could have done what He did for us. He alone receives the glory!

> *"For he hath made him to be sin for us, who knew no sin; that we might be made the righteousness of God in him." (2nd Corinthians 5:21)*

David Recovered All

> *"And there was nothing lacking to them, neither small nor great, neither sons nor daughters, neither spoil, nor any thing that they had taken to them: David recovered all." (1st Samuel 30:19)*

Now that we've related Ziklag's first half to the sufferings of the Son of God let's continue along these same lines to partake of His reward. First, however, we'll summarize David's journey leading up to his miraculous repossession.

> *"And David enquired at the LORD, saying, Shall I pursue after this troop? shall I overtake them? And he answered him, Pursue: for thou shalt surely overtake them, and without fail recover all." (1st Samuel 30:8)*

This exchange between the Lord and David is truly remarkable when taking all things into consideration. After David wept with all his might, he *asked* if he should pursue the troop that just took everything away from him and his people. He put God above his wives, his goods, and well above the fear of his men. Unlike Saul, when facing the pressure to be esteemed in the eyes of his men after spoiling the Amalekites and caved under it… After being spoiled *by* the Amalekites and facing immeasurably more pressure from his men, David feared God!

Consider Saul:

> *"And Saul said unto Samuel, I have sinned: for I have transgressed the commandment of the LORD, and thy words:* ***because I feared the people, and obeyed their voice****." (1st Samuel 15:24) (emphasis mine)*

Prior to this, Saul was told to gather his army and utterly destroy the Amalekites. He was commanded to kill their livestock as well. Nothing was to remain alive! This was because when Israel exited Egypt, the Amalekites laid wait and ambushed the hindermost part of the company. The Lord was repaying them for their iniquity. Sadly, Saul disobeyed the Lord and hearkened to the voice of his men.

All things considered, isn't it interesting how the Amalekites are the same opposing army in each story? In Saul's case, the Amalekites overtook them, but in David's case, he and his men were overtaken. What matters *most*, however, is the response from both men. Only one got it right! Due to David fearing God, he sought the Lord, and the path of life was revealed. The fear of the Lord was David's treasure.

> *"The fear of the LORD tendeth to life: and he that hath it shall abide satisfied; he shall not be visited with evil." (Proverbs 19:23)*

> *"And wisdom and knowledge shall be the stability of thy times, and strength of salvation: the fear of the LORD is his treasure." (Isaiah 33:6)*

Now, we will be discussing fear and love to greater depths in the last chapter, *Perfect Love*, but it is important to distinguish the differences between King Saul and King David. It was *who* they feared. David feared God, and it showed. Contrarily, Saul's life proved he feared all but God.

With that said, consider the encouraging response from the Lord towards David after praying:

> *"And David enquired at the LORD...And he answered him, Pursue: for thou shalt surely overtake them, and without fail recover all." (1st Samuel 30:8)*

How awesome to know beforehand that David would recover everything! David and his six hundred men went to pursue the Amalekites with confidence. However, two hundred of his men were so exhausted they couldn't pass over the brook called Besor, so they stayed behind (1st Samuel 30:9-10).

Afterward, they found an Egyptian in the field who fell sick. He was a slave to an Amalekite who was part of the company that just overtook Ziklag! Coincidence, or not? He hadn't eaten or drank in three days, so the men gave him some much-needed food and water. His spirit then revived in him, and he explained what his company had been up to. David asked if he would take him to the Amalekite encampment, and the Egyptian agreed as long as he wasn't killed for his efforts.

The Word of God depicts David's recovery best when speaking for itself:

> *"And when he had brought him down, behold, they were spread*

abroad upon all the earth, eating and drinking, and dancing, because of all the great spoil that they had taken out of the land of the Philistines, and out of the land of Judah. And David smote them from the twilight even unto the evening of the next day: and there escaped not a man of them, save four hundred young men, which rode upon camels, and fled. And David recovered all that the Amalekites had carried away: and David rescued his two wives." (1st Samuel 30:16-18)

God's Word is so amazing! Consider how two hundred of David's men were so faint that they remained behind while four hundred went on to recover what was stolen. I imagine the four hundred that continued were not much more invigorated than the two hundred that stayed behind. Yet the Bible says that David and his men battled from before sunrise to the next day's evening! If I'm reading this correctly, they battled for a day and a half! To make this even more amazing, the number of men that David came in with was the number of Amalekites that fled away upon camels. This means that David and his four hundred weary men fought at least a few thousand for a day and a half. Wow, God surely fights on His people's behalf!

"And there was nothing lacking to them, neither small nor great, neither sons nor daughters, neither spoil, nor any thing that they had taken to them: ***David [Jesus] recovered all****." (1st Samuel 30:19) (emphasis and brackets mine)*

Now, the repossession of David and his company's wives and goods has ultimately led us to this point. What Jesus reclaimed for us will take us more than one lifetime to fully grasp. However, the way we view Calvary will either propel us forward in obtaining an abundant life here and now or, sadly, only to miss out on all that He paid for. If His death on the cross only pertains to a heaven to come, then we will never perform the greater works He's called us to do on earth.

The Finished Works of Christ

"When Jesus therefore had received the vinegar, he said, ***It is finished****: and he bowed his head, and gave up the ghost." (John 19:30) (emphasis mine)*

This statement right here found in John, *it is finished*, is for the honor of his kings to wholeheartedly grasp. To understand what transpired at redemption is to finally approach the Christian walk correctly. We don't try to catch up to where Jesus left off, but rather we start with Him at the finish line… and go backward!

Go backwards?

…Yes!

Consider this scripture found in Psalms, and allow me to explain:

> *"The law of the LORD is perfect,* ***converting the soul****: the testimony of the LORD is sure, making wise the simple." (Psalm 19:7) (emphasis mine)*

According to the Strong's Concordance, converting means "to turn back, turn to, return; to restore, bring back; to be recovered."

According to the Bible, the Word of God is the only thing that can return our soul back to its original state. To bring our soul back to the Garden where man once walked with God in righteousness. What happened between man's fall and Jesus' finished works at Calvary has shaped our identity thus far. The way we perceive things, the way we make decisions, and the way we experience life, are but a few of the many factors involved concerning our soul.

Though we are born-again, we all in some way have an incomplete picture of the Lord because our soul is like a pair of sunglasses. Everywhere we look, we see life through the perspective of these lenses. Naturally speaking, the darker the tint, the less the sun has an effect on our eyes. Spiritually speaking, the Lord desires us to stare right into the sun with crystal-clear glasses on. Understanding the process of removing the dark tint from the glasses of our soul is contingent upon understanding the finished works of Christ within our perfected spirit.

> *"But we all, with open face beholding as in a glass the glory of the Lord, are changed into the same image from glory to glory, even as by the Spirit of the Lord." (2nd Corinthians 3:18)*

Though He has already finished the works, walking in these truths requires a bit of backtracking. This all pertains to washing our minds with pure water.

Some read the Bible from a place of condemnation. Some read as if we're still in the Old Covenant. Others may be so shaped by the law when reading that the manner of their performance becomes the determining factor of God's love, acceptance, or approval towards them. Some may read the Bible as a "to-do" list instead of an "I did it" list. Reading the Bible is not like a chore list to check off in order to oblige our parents, but rather it is understanding our inheritance granted to us by Christ. We are learning of our new inherited identity as we study! In turn, the water of God's Word *converts* our minds back to our unhindered walk with Him in the Garden. Though we weren't in the original Garden, we're now in a much better one.

Firstly, it is imperative to understand the difference between our soul and our spirit. Our spirit is what has been completely saved and sealed (Ephesians 1:13, Hebrews 10:10, 14, 12:23). This is the Garden in which the Lord dwells! On the other hand, our soul is what is being converted and transformed (Romans 12:2, 2nd Corinthians 4:16, Ephesians 5:26). Our spirit was dead to God via the fall in the Garden, but when Christ said, *"it is finished,"* and we accepted Him as Lord and Savior, we immediately became righteous!

> *"Therefore if any man be in Christ, he is a new creature: old things are passed away; behold, all things are become new." (2nd Corinthians 5:17)*

Notice how it says, "old things are *passed* away," not, "old things are *passing* away." Even so, how can the old things have passed away… when I often battle thinking in the old way? How can I be righteous when I still have unrighteous thoughts? Moreover, how can I justify this next scripture?

> *"For who hath known the mind of the Lord, that he may instruct him?* ***But we have the mind of Christ."*** *(1st Corinthians 2:16) (emphasis mine)*

It surely doesn't seem like I have the mind of Christ when I still think like

David! Well, the scripture is certainly not skewed, nor is there any contradiction in His Word. So, what is the explanation? Do I still have a sinful nature, or have old things passed away? Do I have the mind of Christ or a carnal one? Well, contrary to what most believe, we *do not* have a sinful nature. Old things have passed away, and our spirit has been perfected… *but*… our mind *is* being renewed. The mind of Christ cannot be mistaken with our mind. Our mind must be renewed by His. Where is the mind of Christ? Within our perfected spirit. The mind of Christ is the new man. This new man must become our soul's teacher… and our soul better stand at attention!

Consider the repercussions of man's fall in the Garden. Man was made perfect by God and thrived in his natural habitat. Like a fish is sustained in water, so was man sustained in the Garden by God. Unfortunately, man then disconnected himself from the source of life and has been wandering around aimlessly ever since. Though mankind was still able to communicate with God, it was at the expense of sin and death taking over.

Mankind and the earth itself have been in a state of entropy since the Garden. Man lived nearly a thousand years before physically dying, but after a few thousand years, most are stretching to reach eighty in good health. We have only declined from perfection! Not to mention, we were never meant to die in the first place. Also, the earth was destroyed by a flood, and animals are in perpetual conflict. Sin took its toll! I'm sure I don't have to convince you of the state of the world, but it is important to understand the state of perfection that has decayed *over time*. See, man did not physically die right away. That happened many years later. However, they spiritually died immediately.

In the same way, when we receive Christ, we become righteous immediately! Though the entropic state of man has much backtracking to do to get back to perfection (like a filter being cleansed from all foreign substances), our spirit was perfected the moment we ate from the Tree of Life. This makes a world of difference.

Man is now eating from the Tree of Life, which is Christ. Jesus has restored the paths to dwell in. He has repaired the breach (Isaiah 58:12)! This path that leads back to life is now straight and narrow. Sadly, there are but a few that find it. Now, there aren't many for multiple reasons. When it comes to believers not experiencing the promises of God, the number one reason is ignorance. After reading this book, you will be well aware of the enemy's devices and be well on your way to walking in kingdom authority.

Let me propose a question. What do you suppose is easier… trying to obtain something or defending what was already given? Barring any thought leading us to believe we are ill-equipped to stand our ground, it is certainly easier to hold on to something we already have versus obtaining something we don't. Truly, we have everything we need to confidently stand against the enemy in what we have already inherited. So it is with the finished works of Christ. We are not "hopefully" trying to obtain righteousness through spiritual maturity or God's pleasure based on our performance, but rather we are discovering what we have *already* obtained. Unfortunately, many are not standing their ground in confidence because they don't know what they already have! They are perishing for a lack of knowledge. For this cause, the thief comes to keep us ignorant of what Jesus already accomplished on the cross.

Do you know that thieves come to steal something someone *already* has? Otherwise, what kind of thief are they? Not a good one if they continuously come to an empty house. *This*, my brothers and sisters, is why the thief comes! He comes to stop you from realizing who you have *already* become in Christ. You are a brand-new person! In fact, you are just like Jesus in the spirit (2nd Peter 1:1, 1st John 4:17). Let me assure you, there is an infinite trove of treasure within your heart, and the thief comes after the word that renews your mind to this reality. He knows that if your soul aligns with your spirit… he's lost you and all you confidently come in contact with.

Renew a Right ~~Spirit~~ Within… Soul Within Me!

> *"Create in me a clean heart, O God; and renew a right spirit within me." (Psalm 51:10)*

This Old Testament passage should never be uttered by a New Testament Christian. To speak such a thing would negate the finished works of Christ. (Not to mention, this Psalm was written by David after killing Uriah.) He has already created a new heart within us and has already given us a new spirit. Yet, we sing songs about the Lord doing something He's already done!

> *"A* ***new heart also will I give you****, and* ***a new spirit will I put within you****: and I will take away the stony heart out of your flesh, and I will give you an heart of flesh." (Ezekiel 36:26) (emphasis mine)*

> *"Therefore, if anyone is in Christ,* ***he is a new creation****. The old has passed away; behold,* ***the new has come****." (2nd Corinthians 5:17) (emphasis mine)*

The truth is, we have had a transfer of thrones, but the old king is still vying for its spot. (not our sin nature, which we do not have any longer, but our unrenewed mind) Fortunately, the more we yield ourselves over to the Lord, the more the old king loses his grip. The new King desires to take over the whole kingdom, but some of us limit Him only to the castle. If the castle is the throne room of our heart, then the reach and territory of the kingdom is our whole body. Without coincidence, there is a great portrayal of this kingdom reality for us today found within the lives of Saul, David, and Solomon.

See, our soul was running the show for as long as it could remember, but the Spirit came and took over! It is important to understand that our physical bodies are subject to either living for the flesh or living for the Spirit. Our soul's prior kingdom was subdued and dethroned. Unbeknownst to us, we were held captive by sin and prisoners of the devil until we heard and believed the gospel. Then, the kingdom was given to Saul's… or our *soul's* neighbor: the *spirit*!

> *"And Samuel said unto him, The LORD hath rent the kingdom of Israel from thee* ***this day****, and hath given it to a* ***neighbour of thine, that is better than thou****." (1st Samuel 15:28) (emphasis mine)*

"…That is better than thou." The spirit is greater! The Bible says, *"The elder shall serve the younger"* (Romans 9:12). Regarding our discussion thus far, the "older" soul must now make way for the "younger" spirit. Our born-again spirit is now the one governing the land under the Holy Spirit's direction. Our spirits are now like delegated kings. The spirit is the real you! Our soul's must now line up to this new kingdom order, and in turn, our bodies follow suit.

Why else do you think the Lord said that the kingdom of God is within you? The Father's kingdom is found within each one of His children. He rules from our spirit, but He desires to occupy the whole land. He seeks to establish this new kingdom order (which our spirits have already been revealed) within our souls. The problem is that the soul doesn't give up so easily.

Consider Saul:

> *"And Samuel said unto him, The LORD hath rent the kingdom of Israel from thee* ***this day****... (1st Samuel 15:28) (emphasis mine)*

The Bible says that the kingdom of Israel was taken from Saul *that day*. The sin nature was removed the day we became born-again! We became righteous from day one. Nevertheless… Saul still reigned for forty years!

> *"And afterward they desired a king: and God gave unto them Saul the son of Cis, a man of the tribe of Benjamin,* ***by the space of forty years.****" (Acts 13:21) (emphasis mine)*

Though Saul's power in which to rightfully rule was removed immediately, he didn't leave the picture right away. In fact, it wasn't the Philistines that were David's greatest adversary, but Saul! The same is true for us. The devil has been defeated by the Lord Jesus on the cross. So has our sin nature! He finished the works! Yet the biggest enemy of the Lord today is our unrenewed mind.

> *"Because the carnal mind is enmity [the enemy] against God..." (Romans 8:7)*

Our soul's old order is, in fact, the enemy of God today. Saul was stripped of his throne on the day David was made king, but he still pursued after David to remain in control. Even so, David continuously prevailed:

> *"Now there was long war between the house of Saul and the house of David: but David waxed stronger and stronger, and the house of Saul waxed weaker and weaker." (2nd Samuel 3:1)*

The house of David growing stronger and stronger today is likened unto Jesus' influence within our soul. Adhering to the Word of God will cause the house of Saul, *or our carnal mind*, to diminish. His house continues to grow weaker as the house of David continues to strengthen! See, there were two kings living at the same time in the same land. Only one, however, had the legitimate right to rule.

Saul's influence upon Israel was continuously decreasing. This reminds me of a familiar passage in John:

> *"He must increase, but I must decrease." (John 3:30)*

John the Baptist stated how Jesus' increase would bring his decrease. Similarly, Jesus' increase, or the house of David growing stronger and stronger, automatically brings the house of Saul's decline. Hallelujah! Jesus is our conquering King! Though He finished the works in our spirit, He is conquering the grips of Saul's old order by His Word. This is how Jesus advances His kingdom's rule within the land, which is our body. Moreover, this is how our soul is converted back to Eden.

Concerning Saul: Jesus stripped the flesh of its rule through our carnal soul. (Flesh)

Concerning David: Jesus continually conquers our carnal soul's thinking with His. (Soul)

Concerning Solomon: Jesus rests from war after all our soul's enemies are subdued. (Spirit)

Additionally, David was first anointed king by Samuel in the wilderness. For us, this is as becoming born-again. Though God evidently touched us, we had a long way to go from having a few sheep in the wilderness to all the land subjected to us. Like David had perpetual war with the house of Saul, so do we with our unrenewed minds. Nevertheless, if we fix our eyes upon Jesus in the light of His Word, we eventually make our way to Hebron:

> *And it came to pass after this, that David enquired of the LORD, saying, Shall I go up into any of the cities of Judah? And the LORD said unto him, Go up. And David said, Whither shall I go up? And he said,* ***Unto Hebron****...And the men of Judah came,* ***and there they anointed David king over the house of Judah****... (2nd Samuel 2:1, 4) (emphasis mine)*

The name *Hebron* means *"Place of joining, Alliance."* This is where David was anointed king the second time. In regard to us, Samuel anointing

David king in the wilderness is as our spirit becoming brand new! Then, after a long war with the house of Saul, our soul begins aligning with our spirit. Notice how the men of Judah came and anointed David king. This is significant. See, the men who were initially led by Saul were swayed by David and submitted. This all speaks of the transformation of the soul! The men… *our many thoughts and opinions that proceed from our souls…* are finally joining with David! Though it is only Judah that came to this procession, it is this line (Judah) that Jesus came through. In regard to us, this is where we have completely submitted to the kingship of Christ. He is not only Savior but He has been accepted as Lord.

"Can two walk together, except they be agreed?" (Amos 3:3)

We now begin to walk in agreement with Him. This long war has led us to our soul's submission. Now to walk it out! This is where His finished works have not only been accepted but have begun to take over. The land is evidently under new order by the fruits of our conversations and thought life. We are seeing things differently and are thinking in ways that coincide with faith and the kingdom of God. We have allowed Him to take over the land.

Finally, the next step over the threshold is where Jesus desires for all to arrive. Unfortunately, few are found to be walking in such a way. This next procession is where all the other tribes submit as well. If our thoughts are likened unto the people, Jesus has fully persuaded them all! No opposition!

> *"Then came all the tribes of Israel to David unto Hebron, and spake, saying, Behold, we are thy bone and thy flesh...**So all the elders** of Israel came to the king to Hebron; and king David made a league with them in Hebron before the LORD: **and they anointed David king over Israel**." (2nd Samuel 5:1, 3) (emphasis mine)*

This is the fruit of Jesus' labor. A bride who is suitable for Himself. One that looks just like Him! One who is equally yoked! This is not a hostile takeover. It is one of surrender through the will of the people. Jesus desires for all the *elders* (or older of the land) to be fully persuaded of Him (all our old ways to be changed), not in Judah alone, but in all of Israel. The elder shall serve the younger! This is typological of Jesus having full reign over and through us. No aspect of the house of Saul hindering His work. Not Saul nor his children. Even Michal was barren! David's wife, the daughter of Saul, could not produce children for him—no conception of the old kingdom's order. Moreover, the only son left of Saul's house to consider is Mephibosheth, which is crippled. Thus, *"David"* reigns with absolute authority.

> *"And David perceived that the LORD had established him king over Israel, and that he had exalted his kingdom for his people Israel's sake." (2nd Samuel 5:12)*

This makes way for Solomon:

> *"Then Solomon sat on the throne of the LORD as king instead of David his father, and prospered; and all Israel obeyed him." (1st Chronicles 29:23)*

> *"So king Solomon was king over all Israel." (1st Kings 4:1)*

Solomon ruling from a position of peace is as Jesus ruling through us without any obstruction. This is His desire… to walk with us as he did with Adam without anything coming in between. Though we sinned, we have been restored. Though there is a devil that still seeks to devour, our souls are fully persuaded of who we are in Christ, and who Christ is in us. We aren't ignorant to his devices, nor do we ever give him place. We are clothed in righteousness and suited in God's armor. The sword of the Spirit is sharp and swift in our hands.

Let us now discuss one of the "tribes" that need to be persuaded in order to walk in agreement with God's will. Truthfully, this kingdom principle is hard to be convinced of. Jesus has long war with this train of thought.

Forget Not All His Benefits

It is most important to preface how one subsection of a chapter can never discuss the depths of healing in full. For this, I recommend one of the greatest books on divine healing out there today. It's titled, *"Christ The Healer"* by F.F. Bosworth.

> *"Bless the LORD, O my soul: and all that is within me, bless his holy name. Bless the LORD, O my soul, and* ***forget not all his benefits****: Who*

> ***forgiveth all*** *thine iniquities; who* ***healeth all*** *thy diseases; Who redeemeth thy life from destruction; who crowneth thee with lovingkindness and tender mercies; Who satisfieth thy mouth with good things; so that thy youth is renewed like the eagle's." (Psalm 103:1-5) (emphasis mine)*

Jesus forgave us and healed us *totally…* whether we feel like it or not! We must receive it by faith according to His Word. It is our inheritance! The process of renewing, or recovering that which was lost, is the journey of a believer. There was no sickness in the Garden of Eden, and we've been translated into a better one. Psalm 103 is an Old Testament promise of being forgiven and delivered… how much more does it now pertain to us under the New Covenant?

As mentioned prior, it is easier to stand our ground in something we have already obtained than to seek something not already owned. If Isaiah 53 is true, and if 1st Peter 2:24 is true as well, *which it is…* then what are we missing if we still suffer from sickness? Well, in accordance to standing our ground in something obtained… divine health is one of those things!

Remember the example of the thief? Well, he is coming to steal divine health from you by *placing* sickness upon you! He is stealing health from you. Most Christians, when sick, pray for the Lord to heal them instead of rebuking the illegal symptoms. Some would go as far as to say that if not healed, it must not have been God's will. Brethren, it is *always* God's will to heal… because He has *already* healed us!

> *"**Who hath believed our report?** and to whom is the arm of the LORD revealed?...Surely he hath borne our **griefs**, and carried our **sorrows**: yet we did esteem him stricken, smitten of God, and afflicted. But he was wounded for our transgressions, he was bruised for our iniquities: the chastisement of our peace was upon him; and with his stripes **we are healed**." (Isaiah 53:1, 4-5) (emphasis mine)*

Do you believe His report? The word *griefs* in Hebrew is translated to *sicknesses* and *diseases*, and the word *sorrows* translates to *pains*. He bore our sicknesses and pains!

Jesus fulfilled Isaiah's prophecy irrefutably when he healed the sick during His earthly ministry. He then ultimately bore our sin and sickness upon the cross at the end of it. Isaiah 53 could not be pertaining to the spiritual alone, which some believe because the scripture states in Matthew how he fulfilled it when he *physically* healed the people:

> *"When the even was come, they brought unto him many that were possessed with devils: and he cast out the spirits with his word, and* ***healed all that were sick****: That it might be fulfilled which was* ***spoken by Esaias the prophet****, saying, Himself took our* ***infirmities****, and bare our* ***sicknesses****." (Matthew 8 :16-17) (emphasis mine)*

Some may say, "If that's the case, then why does 1st Peter 2:24 only say He bore our sins on the cross, and not sicknesses?"

> *"Who his own self* ***bare our sins*** *in his own body on the tree, that we, being dead to sins, should live unto righteousness: by whose stripes* ***ye were healed****." (1st Peter 2:24) (emphasis mine)*

Well… where did sickness come from?

We have been delivered from death, which came by sin. Sickness is not greater than sin because sin is the root. The fruits of sickness and disease came from the root of sin. This is precisely why when Jesus healed the paralytic, He told him that his sins were forgiven and to rise up and walk. This man was physically paralyzed, but it stemmed from sin in the first place. Of course, the Pharisees and religious leaders went mad over this! Jesus perceiving their thoughts, asked, *"What's easier to say, your sins are forgiven, or rise and walk?"* (Matthew 9:5). Jesus was basically saying, *"What's the difference?"*

Now, one could argue that it is easier to say your sins are forgiven rather than rise up and walk because one is unseen, and the other is seen, which I would agree with. However, one could also make a case for Jesus implying how it was one in the same. Jesus was making it known that the forgiveness of sin is synonymous with being healed in your body. This is one of the things that Jesus recovered: our health!

Along the lines with much of our discussion thus far, consider this passage from the one whom Jesus loved:

> *"Beloved, I wish above all things that thou mayest prosper and be in health, even as thy soul prospereth." (3rd John 2)*

The contingency here is a prosperous soul. The water of God's Word washes our mind and clarifies the heavenly will of God. Just as much as there is no sickness in the kingdom of God, so it should be with the citizens of that kingdom here on earth. A prosperous soul will cause a prosperous body to materialize.

Consider this passage:

> *"A sound [whole] heart is the life of the flesh..." (Proverbs 14:30) (brackets mine)*

When our soul and spirit are in harmony, the body follows suit. We have been translated into a heavenly kingdom; therefore, thinking in a heavenly manner is vital. Regardless of how it looks, feels, or seems, the truth is, "by His stripes we *were* healed" (1st Peter 2:24).

Now, the Bible says to speak to the mountain, and it will be removed. Let me stop there for a moment and ask you this: do you believe that? Do you *really* believe that? First of all, do you believe that sickness is a mountain? If so, what happens when you don't see it removed? Is it God's fault? Or worse yet, is the scripture not true?

> *"For verily I say unto you, That whosoever shall say unto this mountain, Be thou removed, and be thou cast into the sea; and shall not doubt in his heart, but shall believe that those things which he saith shall come to pass; he shall have whatsoever he saith. Therefore I say unto you, What things soever ye desire, when ye pray, believe that ye receive them, and ye shall have them." (Mark 11:23-24)*

According to the gospel of Mark, the mountain being removed is dependent upon speaking in faith *without* doubt. Some speak to God *about* the mountain, but all the while, within, they are uncertain. Then, some wonder if it's always God's will to heal if their prayer goes "unanswered." They think, *"Surely, I must have been in faith! I prayed, and prayed, and prayed!"* Though faith is faith before the baby is delivered into your hands, we cannot say we were in faith without *eventually* holding the delivered child. Faith sees the child delivered before… but will stand fast until it's tangibly held. This is why it's imperative to know God's will altogether. One who doesn't see through until the end is either misinformed of their inherited rights, allowed doubt to abort the process, or worse yet… they never saw it in the first place. Faith is the *manifestation* of our hope (Hebrews 11:1). So, where are we placing our hope?

> *"Hope deferred maketh the heart sick: but when the desire cometh, it is a tree of life." (Proverbs 13:12)*

Deferred Hope

It will help to mention a time when I allowed my hope to become deferred. Instead of my heart being whole and providing life to all my flesh (Proverbs 14:30), my heart became sick and yielded sickness as a result (Proverbs 13:12).

Now, imagine going to a doctor and explaining how you had the flu or suffered from arthritis or any one of the countless diseases and disorders out there, and he were to say, *"Ok, well how's your heart?"* You may wonder why you ever allowed him to diagnose you! Nevertheless, this is a kingdom reality. When it comes to our bodies falling subject to sicknesses and pain… truly, it is a matter of the heart.

Nearly all of us believe germs have a natural place over our mortal bodies as Christians. I beg to differ. It is not germs that are allowed through our skin, mouth, or eyes… but the fear of those germs allowed through an unguarded heart. I know this is shocking, but it is the truth! Through unbelief, doubt, and fear, we untether our hope from the source of Life and allow the assignment of the thief to prevail. It was not his victory but rather our loss. We concede and allow sickness to have a place through an open door of the heart. This door is opened through fear, and then whatever natural or demonic disease that was knocking is welcomed in.

Truly, germs do not have the right to make us sick, as much as temptation has the right to make us sin. It is only through the conception of these things in our minds that we give birth. This might be a radical statement to you! You may want to pause and ask the Holy Spirit to reveal these truths if they are unfamiliar. If you don't want to give me the benefit of the doubt, ask

Him!

How else do you believe you're immune from poisonous drinks? I assure you if a poisonous drink enters your mouth, but fear enters your heart… the promise is null and void. It is not the promise that didn't work, but your heart in which deferred the hope of that promise. Moreover, ignorance will not stop the poison's effects. Only faith will. Ignorance will kill you just as quickly as fear. Let me make a bold yet simple statement: if we were wholeheartedly convinced that sickness had no right, we wouldn't ever be sick!

With that said, I will highlight a time where I allowed sickness to have place in my body. Though I regret not guarding my heart with all diligence, I am grateful for the manner in which I was recompensed because it pertains greatly to this chapter.

I was working with a contractor at the time who unknowingly had covid. This was when it first came around. He called me after going for a test the next day and said he had it. I must admit, fear came against me. I was working as a young adult leader in a particular church at the time and thought, *"What will everyone think if I get covid after I've been ministering to them on healing?* I was not afraid of the repercussions of the flu; I was afraid of losing my witness. I was afraid of looking like a hypocrite.

Unfortunately, the headache, body aches, and fever set in that night. Regardless of what anyone may think, I know I allowed this demonic sickness to have place through fear. Truthfully, we never have to be sick! Though it was mild, and most of the time, I rebuked the fever and headache and gained relief, I ultimately conceded to the sickness altogether.

After a week into it, I lost my taste and smell. I recovered relatively quickly, but my taste and smell were still missing. In fact, I went over a month without tasting or smelling. Interestingly, when I was younger and was asked what I wanted to be when I grew up, I responded with, *"I want to be a perfume smeller!"* I don't know how great it pays, but I would still be interested in such a position.

With that said, I was finished with not being able to smell or taste anything. I finally had enough. So, in faith, I declared, *"I command my scent and taste to return to me! It is my scent, and it is my taste, and I command you, thief, to return it to me at once!"* That night I had a dream of David in

Ziklag and how he recovered all. I awoke to have a cup of coffee with both the taste and the smell of it. It was without coincidence that my senses returned to me that next day in full. It was faith in God's Word that:

> *"...this is the confidence that we have in him, that, if we ask any thing according to his will, he heareth us." (1st John 5:14)*

Only those who know His will can ask in confidence.

That By These!

> *"Whereby are given unto us exceeding great and precious promises: **that by these** ye might be partakers of the divine nature, having escaped the corruption that is in the world through lust." (2nd Peter 1:4)*

That by these... that by these what? The exceeding great and precious promises! Through these promises, we partake of the divine nature. We must exercise our rights by meditating on what His Word says. We prove His Word by standing our ground despite the relentless contradictions (Hebrews 12:3). We must never go by how we feel but only by what the Word of God says. This is precisely why the enemy attacks by saying, *"Has God said"*? He knows that if he can make you question what God said, you'll always consider how you feel.

With that said, here are some of those exceeding great and precious promises:

> *"These things I have spoken unto you, that in me ye might have peace. In the world ye shall have tribulation: **but be of good cheer; I have overcome the world**." (John16:33) (emphasis mine)*

He has overcome the world! Though we have difficulties, our God has *already* won!

> *"**Peace I leave with you**, my peace I give unto you: not as the world giveth, give I unto you. Let not your heart be troubled, neither let it be afraid." (John 14:27) (emphasis mine)*

He gave us His peace!

> *"Let your conversation be without covetousness; and be content with such things as ye have: for he hath said,* ***I will never leave thee, nor forsake thee****." (Hebrews 13:5) (emphasis mine)*

> *"Teaching them to observe all things whatsoever I have commanded you: and, lo,* ***I am with you always****, even unto the end of the world. Amen." (Matthew 28:20) (emphasis mine)*

He is with us always and He will never leave us!

> *"For I will be merciful to their unrighteousness, and their sins and their iniquities will I remember no more." (Hebrews 8:12)*

He has totally removed our sins!

> *"As far as the east is from the west, so far hath he removed our transgressions from us." (Psalm 103:12)*

> *"And their sins and iniquities will I remember no more." (Hebrews 10:17)*

We are forgiven. You are forgiven!

> *"Surely he hath borne our griefs, and carried our sorrows: yet we did esteem him stricken, smitten of God, and afflicted. But he was wounded for our transgressions, he was bruised for our iniquities: the chastisement of our peace was upon him; and with his stripes we are healed." (Isaiah 53:4, 5)*

> *"Who his own self bare our sins in his own body on the tree, that we, being dead to sins, should live unto righteousness: by whose stripes ye were healed." (1st Peter 2:24)*

Our God has healed us!
Most importantly… Our God loves us!

> *"For the Father himself loveth you, because ye have loved me, and have believed that I came out from God." (John 16:27)*

Now, it is impossible to discuss all the promises of God in this chapter, but there is a fantastic book out there I highly recommend. It is one of a kind and is truly inspired. It's called the Bible! I encourage you to read the Bible in the light I strove to convey. The New Testament is meant to be read just as its title states: *a covenant, a will, an inheritance.* If you read the Bible as one would read a will from a passing relative, you'd be well on your way. Grace and peace to you in the discovery of your inheritance!

7

Smoothed Stones

"And he took his staff in his hand, and chose him five ***smooth stones out of the brook,*** *and put them in a shepherd's bag which he had, even in a scrip; and his sling was in his hand: and he drew near to the Philistine." (1st Samuel 17:40) (emphasis mine)*

Each chapter thus far has stayed true to the theme and purpose of this book. There has been one goal in mind throughout our journey. It is simply, and most wonderfully this: to see Jesus, *God's glory*, revealed throughout the lives of these Old Testament kings as we, His New Testament *kings*, seek Him out.

From His parable's concealing the glory of His word, to the gospel concealed through three consecutive chapters in the book of Samuel; from David and Bathsheba's firstborn son being slain, to Jesus' temple being destroyed in order for us to be restored; from Solomon's Temple being filled with God's glory, to the gospel revealed through David's pressings in Ziklag: Jesus is the matter we've been searching (Proverbs 25:2).

The Bible says, *"As He is, so are we in this world"* (1st John 4:17). God has called us to behold Him. In doing so, *"We change from glory to glory"* (2nd Corinthians 3:18). Therefore, the more we see Him, the more we become like Him. The more we walk towards Him, the more we are able to walk like Him. This is why we've relentlessly sought for Him these past six chapters.

With that said, one of the fruits of beholding God's glory is to do the works that He has done. He told us that we would (John 14:12). The next two chapters will focus on God's power and love. We will start with the power of the tongue in this chapter and finish with love in the last. For truly, the greatest of these is love.

Let us now discuss how to apply the proven word in battle. Understanding this kingdom principle is paramount to our success. Though we live in a physical world, our weapons are not (2nd Corinthians 10:4). David's weaponry may have been a sling and a stone, but his harp and song enabled him to stand before Goliath.

When it comes to our fight, we must understand how to battle God's way. God calls us to stand in His armament, with our feet shod in preparation. In preparation of what? In preparation of *Him*. He is the good news!

Moreover, our greatest weapon is knowledge. More specifically, the knowledge of Who He is and Who He is in us. Truly, the truth sets us free. However, it is not the truth alone but the truth we *know* that sets us free. The Bible says that we perish for a lack of knowledge (Hosea 4:6). We can succumb to the enemy's tactics when we fall short of knowing who we surely are in Christ. In essence, our greatest weapon is our relationship with the Word and understanding our current position. Unquestionably, this truth is what enabled David to prevail against the giant.

This chapter will focus on the root of David's success against Goliath. Comprehending the spiritual truths at play will modernize this famous battle and reveal a deep yet practical relation for us today. Faith, hope, and love will become evident when breaking down the steps leading to the giant's fall. A behind-the-scenes look at David's life will reveal the most beautiful depiction of God's proven system for us to follow.

David wasn't preparing to fight giants per se. The giant's fall was merely a casualty of his relationship with God.

The Flowing Brook

> *"So then faith cometh by hearing, and hearing by the Word of God" (Romans 10:17)*

To preface this subsection, it is important to note that faith comes by hearing. Though this scripture found in Romans more specifically applies to hearing the gospel and receiving the initial faith to believe for salvation, it can also relate to honing our spiritual ears to be built up in faith over fear. Truly, we can build our faith by hearing faith to begin with. So, when we speak the Word of God, we hear the promises. We distinguish the kingdom truths over the worldly doubts and lies. Though we can spiritually hear without utterance, for instance, silently reading the Bible (which is the most common form of renewing our minds), it is of utmost importance to also consistently declare the promises out loud. We don't need to have a Bible in our hands to meditate, but the promises being declared from our mouths out of our hearts over and again will prove to compound the effect. To meditate is to be fruitful and multiply in the Lord. To meditate is to smooth out the stones for the slings of our tongues. This is the kingdom preparation of a New Covenant soldier.

> *"But his delight is in the law of the LORD; and in his law doth he **meditate** day and night. And he shall be like a tree planted by the **rivers of water**, that bringeth forth his fruit in his season; his leaf also shall not wither; and whatsoever he doeth shall prosper." (Psalms 1:2-3) (emphasis mine)*

Seeking for, finding, and learning of Jesus is our highest call and greatest honor. Not to study to preach a good sermon, not to memorize and quote scripture, but to *meditate* on Christ Himself. This will ground us in love and will inevitably be the key to our success.

This may surprise you, but the biblical definition of *meditate*, as found in Joshua 1:8, means to *utter a sound* or *thoughtful deliberation with the implication of speaking to oneself: meditation.*

> *"This book of the law shall not depart **out of thy mouth**; but thou shalt **meditate** therein day and night, that thou mayest observe to do according to all that is written therein: for then thou shalt make thy way prosperous, and then thou shalt have good success." (Joshua 1:8) (emphasis mine)*

The world's definition of meditation is to empty your mind and to be silent, but God's definition is to fill it and to speak. More specifically, to fill it with *Him*!

> *"Thou wilt keep him in perfect peace, whose **mind is stayed on thee**: because he trusteth in thee." (Isaiah 26:3) (emphasis mine)*

> *"My meditation of **him** shall be sweet: I will be glad in the LORD." (Psalm 104:34) (emphasis mine)*

Nevertheless, you can fill your mind and mouth with scripture and still not see the heart behind the letter. The Pharisees excelled at this. The scriptures are not solely meant to be studied to preach a substantive message but to be diligently meditated upon to know God personally.

For instance, one may have memorized key components of textbooks and ultimately passed a test to become a professional in their desired field. However, would that individual have meditated upon the author of those textbooks or only the text? This was the problem with the Pharisees and Sadducees. They failed to know the Author! They may have known the Author's words but not the Author's heart:

> *"Search the scriptures; for in them ye think ye have eternal life: and they are they which testify of me." (John 5:39)*

Now, I am confident that you nor I am a Pharisee, but we can easily fall into similar traps if not aware. Here is a solid principle to learn: we should never study scripture only to teach but to be taught. Moreover, we should rarely, if ever, be studying scripture to put together a message. We should be studying scripture to *know* Him and to *become* the message! When we seek the Teacher to show us His ways, we will then have no problem sharing with others from the overflow. Moses is an excellent example:

> *"He made known his ways unto Moses, his acts unto the children of Israel." (Psalm 103:7)*

Moses knew His ways, the Children of Israel only His acts.

> *"Show me Thy ways, O Lord; teach me Thy paths." (Psalm 25:4)*

When He is found, learning of God's ways is the honor of kings. It is the point of our pursuit! See, the children of Israel knew *what* God did, but Moses knew *why* he did it. Not to imply Moses fully comprehended the mind and heart of God Almighty, I hope this would have gone without saying… but only to shed light on the reason why Moses was so successful: *Moses was intimate with God.*

In Moses's quiet time with the Lord, he was revealed things the Children of Israel never were. He began to see His motives. Though he saw what the Children of Israel saw, and though he heard what they heard, Moses first saw and heard God's heart behind it.

This is the recurring theme with any prominent biblical figure the Lord used. Seeking after God's heart is what distinguished them from the rest.

Amongst the twelve disciples, John the beloved comes to mind when leaning on Jesus' chest at Passover to hear His heartbeat. Mary sitting at Jesus' feet and later anointing them with costly perfume and wiping them down with her hair was the fruit of her genuine love! I'm even reminded of the ten lepers being healed, yet only one returning to give God praise and thanks. This all speaks of seeking the Word behind the word.

Like Moses and those mentioned, King David was a man after God's own heart. This is what enabled him to prosper in all his ways. Undoubtedly, knowing God was the key to his success. David's worship and meditation upon the Lord in the wilderness set him apart from the Israelites, who feared when faced with the giant.

Giant Words

> *"When Saul and all Israel heard those words of the Philistine, they were dismayed, and greatly afraid." (1st Samuel 17:11)*

Fear is a symptom of a lack of intimacy with God. One who fears is not made perfect in God's love (1st John 4:18). The Philistine's words struck fear in the core of all Israel, including King Saul. All, but one, was afraid:

> *"And as he talked with them, behold, there came up the champion, the Philistine of Gath, Goliath by name, out of the armies of the Philistines,* ***and spake according to the same words: and David heard them.****" (1st Samuel 17:23) (emphasis mine)*

Interestingly, David overheard Goliath speaking the exact same words Israel heard. However, he heard them differently than everyone else. Why? Because David was more familiar with God's words than the words of the stranger. He *meditated* upon God's Word.

David knew the enemy was not Goliath but the words he uttered. No matter his stature, he spoke in contradiction to the covenant David had with God. For this cause, David was provoked to action. Goliath's words simply didn't line up with God's. Therefore, he had to be taken out.

This battle that we find ourselves in is one of words.

> *"...and David* ***heard*** *them. And all the men of Israel,* ***when they saw the man****, fled from him, and were sore afraid. And the men of Israel said,* ***Have ye seen this man*** *that is come up?..." (1st Samuel 17:23-25) (emphasis mine)*

As we will soon see, the way David responded to the giant's words, versus the way Israel did, revealed the root of his courage. He wasn't afraid because He was overflowing in the love of God!

> *"There is no fear in love; but perfect love casteth out fear: because fear hath torment. He that feareth is not made perfect in love." (1st John 4:18)*

Love wasn't only doctrinal with David, it was personal. His courageous response reflected the depth of his relationship with God Almighty.

> *"...For out of the abundance of the heart the mouth speaketh." (Matthew 12:34)*

Take notice also to the wording previously mentioned in first Samuel: David *heard...* the Israelites *saw*. The Israelites were led by their eyes, but David, his ears. We walk by faith, not by sight (2nd Corinthians 5:7). Had the Israelites heard God the way David did, they would have seen the giant the way David did!

This relates to us more than we know. Our response to whatever giant appears in our lives is indicative of the relationship we have with the Word of God. If we respond in fear, it is because of a lack of intimacy with the Word. If we respond in faith, it is the fruit of a healthy relationship with Jesus.

> *But the* ***fruit of the Spirit*** *is love, joy, peace, longsuffering, gentleness, goodness,* ***faith****, Meekness, temperance: against such there is no law." (Galatians 5:22, 23) (emphasis mine)*

Faith is a fruit! David's faith-filled response to Goliath was the result of his time spent in the wilderness alone with God. He had only heard truth from his Father, day in and day out! He spent his days worshipping on his harp, praying, and meditating upon the Lord. David was built up in faith because he abided in God's love (Jude 20, 21).

> *"...but faith which worketh by love." (Galatians 5:6)*

If we are rooted and grounded in God's love and His Word, faith is a naturally supernatural response to the giants that lie ahead. This is God's perfect will for our lives. Like David, we shouldn't see Goliath, we should only hear a contradiction to our covenant with God.

> *"And the Philistine said, I defy the armies of Israel this day..." (1st Samuel 17:10)*

Take notice of David's bold response:

> *"...for who is this uncircumcised Philistine, that he should **defy** the armies of the living God?" (1st Samuel 17:26) (emphasis mine)*

What happens when someone tries to defy the law? Someone may/should say, *"I know my rights!"* How can someone know their rights, without knowing the law? Truly, there are kingdom laws that supersede earthly laws through faith.

By Faith... You have the right to be physically healed (Isaiah 53:4, 5, 1st Peter 2:24, Matthew 8:17). You have the right to a sound mind, and to prosper even as your soul prospers (2nd Timothy 1:7, 3rd John 2). Moreover, you have the right to Peace (Isaiah 9:6, 26:3, John 14:27). Despite all contradicting circumstances, you have the right to remain in joy and in God's unfailing love (Galatians 5:22, 23). You are immune to poisonous drinks, venomous snakes, deadly plagues, and infectious diseases (Mark 16:18, Psalm 91). You have authority over all the works of the devil (Luke 10:19). These are but a few of our many God-given rights through Christ!

> *"...for who is this **uncircumcised** Philistine..." (1st Samuel 17:26)*

David responded out of right, not sight. He knew the Word of God. That's why he said, *"Who is this uncircumcised [without covenant] Philistine?"* In other words, *"What right does he have?"* We too can respond to the giants that lie ahead through covenantal right. Truly, this is the sum of this chapter in full... this is the honor of kings! When the intruder comes to provoke, accuse, condemn, or to steal, we have every right to confidently stand our kingdom ground in faith, regardless of what it looks like.

Prepare The Way

On a brief historical sidenote, it is appropriate, and necessary even, to discuss the growth of Saul's army compared to that of David's. This will tie closely to the *acts* Israel saw versus the *ways* Moses experienced. As John, Mary, and the leper who were made whole stood out amongst their company, so will David stand out amongst his brothers.

Concerning Saul and his army, the only two initially found in Israel with a sword were Saul and Jonathan. Due to the Philistines conquering Israel in the prophet Eli's time and capturing the Ark of the Covenant, Israel's military capability was greatly diminished. Insomuch there was not a blacksmith found throughout all their land, but only a file for the militia to sharpen their farming tools to use as weapons (1st Samuel 13:19-21).

> *"So it came to pass in the day of battle, that there was neither sword nor spear found in the hand of any of the people that were with Saul and Jonathan: but with Saul and with Jonathan his son was there found." (1st Samuel 13:22)*

In 1st Samuel 13, we find that Saul inherited a small militia scarcely equipped for battle. They were nowhere near the army they would soon become.

However, the following chapter reveals the tides instantaneously turning. This initiated when Jonathan and his armourbearer decided to climb the enemy's garrison and attack the Philistines. They received a sign from the Lord to advance and slew twenty of the Philistine soldiers! From this, God instilled fear and sent an earthquake into the surrounding host of the Philistines, which ultimately led to them killing each other with their own swords!

> *"...And, behold, the multitude melted away, and they went on beating down one another...And Saul and all the people that were with him assembled themselves, and they came to the battle: and, behold, every man's sword was against his fellow...So the LORD saved Israel that day..." (1st Samuel 14:16, 20, 23)*

This was the beginning of Saul's army gaining territory, numbers, and perhaps the most timely and important: swords! The swords that were once held within the hands of the enemy, were now held within the hands of Israel. In a moment, the Lord equipped Saul's army for battle.

> *"So Saul took the kingdom over Israel, and fought against all his enemies on every side, against Moab, and against the children of Ammon, and against Edom, and against the kings of Zobah, and against the Philistines: and whithersoever he turned himself, he vexed them. And he gathered an host, and smote the Amalekites, and delivered Israel out of the hands of them that spoiled them." (1st Samuel 14:47-48)*

Saul and his army were now gaining ground, experience, and confidence in their effectiveness as soldiers. Though God was the means behind each victory, it may not have been as evident, or rather intimate, to Israel as God would have wanted it. In speculation, I believe they were mostly relying in their newfound confidence as "Saul's army." Goliath's appearance would prove where their confidence ultimately lied.

Now, David's preparation was worlds apart from that of Saul's army. His brothers were soldiers of Saul, but he himself was a shepherd. He spent his time in the wilderness with sheep, not with the soldiers. David had no prior military experience when confronted with Goliath, but he had experience, nonetheless.

His experience stemmed from the supernatural. Though I am confident he was proficient with a sling, it was not his sling that secured his victory against the giant. Nor was it his sling that killed the lion and bear when they stole from his flock (1st Samuel 17:34-35). Remember, this was an up-close encounter (he grabbed the bear and the lion by its hair, then struck and killed it). A sling wouldn't even have worked! It was the Spirit of God upon David that enabled him to destroy beasts much larger and more powerful than himself. We now have that same Spirit!

Surely the details of David's life were written for our example. In seeking the kingdom of God and His righteousness *first*, David was revealed how to battle God's way. This is a major reason why David refused to fight with Saul's equipment, which we will soon discuss.

> *"Blessed be the LORD my strength, which teacheth my hands to war, and my fingers to fight: My goodness, and my fortress; my high tower, and my deliverer; my shield, and he in whom I trust..." (Psalm 144:1-2)*

In addition, David was not gaining ground geographically nor gathering up spoils from his slain enemies. Nevertheless, he surely gained more ground and treasure than any soldier of Saul. He was gaining ground in the spirit and gathering up the riches of wisdom, knowledge, and understanding. He was becoming more and more proficient in his walk with God through worship, praise, and meditating on the word. This would prove to be the more effective training.

In fact, the scripture describes David as a man of war *before* he faced Goliath:

> *"...Behold, I have seen a son of Jesse the Bethlehemite, that is cunning in playing, and a mighty valiant man, and a* ***man of war****, and prudent in matters, and a comely person, and the LORD is with him." (1st Samuel 16:18) (emphasis mine)*

This is remarkable! David was shepherding sheep yet was called a man of war! Due to the obvious fact that David wasn't a soldier of Saul, this servant must have seen past his current profession. Truly, he was seeing in the spirit.

David was about to bring his private relationship with God public.

To that point, consider this: David's first encounter with Saul was that of deliverance! It was *spiritual* warfare. David was asked to play his harp to deliver the king from the evil spirit that troubled him (1st Samuel 16:14-23). This was the man of war the servant beheld. This is what David was prepared for.

> *"For we wrestle not against flesh and blood, but against principalities, against powers, against the rulers of darkness of this world, against spiritual wickedness in high places." (Ephesians 6:12)*

Important to note that David wasn't so much playing his harp for Saul but for the Lord. His worship unto God brought deliverance unto Saul. In other words, the fruit of his relationship with God set Saul free! Like those in the Philippian jail were set free by Paul and Silas' praise unto the Lord, so was Saul set free by David's.

This is also true for us: our freedom in Christ will bring freedom to the captives. For this cause, walking in love and not fear is of the utmost importance. Being rooted and grounded in love will bear fruit to the fearful, so they may taste and see that God is good! Fear should never grip us, but only the hands of this needy world for the fruits of God's Holy Spirit.

This can only occur by following David's training regimen, not Saul's. See, those who followed Saul may have looked the part, but David acted the part when it mattered. For truly, all seems well until Goliath shows up.

Consider this, how many people in church have walked away when leadership fell? How many lives were bound up in following their leader and not Christ? Was most of their Christianity based on a weekly gathering around a gift, or was it founded on their daily walk with Christ?

Moreover, how many of us consider our leadership as our main source of biblical ministration? In other words, are we diving daily into the Word for ourselves to learn who God is? If we look at Sunday service as our main source of learning, we won't stand a chance against Goliath.

I say this in love… but whether through ignorance, fear, or complacency, some have a form of godliness but deny the transformative power of the Lord. There might be some outward growth but no true inward growth. Christianity then becomes limited to mere behavior modification rather than supernatural transformation. Some of us are comfortable with the morality and the tradition of Christianity, so long as we are seeing battle after battle won with our newfound swords, but once a giant appears, we quickly faint.

Our confidence must stem from a personal, daily walk with Jesus Christ, and our preparation must be that of true worship unto God and the meditation of His Word. This is the *only* way to stand against a giant.

Battle Tested

For he had not proved it…

Now, before David sunk a stone into Goliath's forehead, there was a crucial conversation he had with Saul beforehand. Had David listened to Saul, we wouldn't be speaking of him today.

> *"And Saul armed David with his armour, and he put an helmet of brass upon his head; also he armed him with a coat of mail. And David girded his sword upon his armour, and he* ***assayed [to be bold]*** *to go;* ***for he had not proved it.*** *And David said unto Saul, I cannot go with these; for I have not proved them.* ***And David put them off him.****" (1st Samuel 17:38-39) (emphasis and brackets mine)*

Concerning the phrase *"proved it"* in this passage, David was saying that Saul's armor was not battle-tested for himself. He hadn't ever fought "Saul's" way. Therefore, he wasn't confident with it. Interestingly, David's armor was proven more effective, though he didn't wear any.

Notwithstanding, who wouldn't want to yield the king's sword? Who wouldn't want to be arrayed in the king's armor? Saul must have slain thousands with that sword! However, David's trust in his own preparations prevailed.

In relation to us, oftentimes we are more considerate of the way others fight their battles than we are of our own. This may be more of a common problem in the church than we might be aware of. The reason being that we see and hear the powerful testimonies from our leaders or through television and books of others in the body of Christ but perhaps have seen little success of our own.

The way others speak, or have seen success, is attractive because we want to achieve similar results! However, we could be striving to live vicariously through the warfare that was proven for them but not yet for us. David put off Saul's armor from him because he wasn't familiar with it. And truth be told, had he faced Goliath in Saul's armor, he would have been killed.

Consider the seven sons of Sceva. They tried to fight the way Paul was accustomed to:

> *"...* ***We adjure you by Jesus whom Paul preacheth****. And there were seven sons of one Sceva, a Jew, and chief of the priests, which did so. And the evil spirit answered and said,* ***Jesus I know, and Paul I know; but who are ye****? And the man in whom the evil spirit was leaped on*

them, and overcame them, and prevailed against them, so that they fled out of that house naked and wounded." (Acts 19:13-16) (emphasis mine)

The sons of Sceva tried to battle the enemy the way Paul had seen success! Of course, this didn't work because it was proven for Paul but wasn't yet proven for them. They were overcome, wounded, and ultimately fled the scene in shame. Though this is a considerably extreme example, it certainly holds significant value. It proves it is not merely "quoting" scripture but rather a deep and bold relationship with Jesus through biblical meditation. It is our *faith* that the enemy responds to. *"Paul, I know…Jesus, I know"*. Knowing God for ourselves produces boldness!

To be clear, this is not to say we should wait to apply biblical principles that leaders in the body of Christ reveal. Truth is truth! This is only to say we cannot expect their results to be hurried for us. They may have meditated on those passages for years! Like Joshua, they may have seen prosperity and success (Joshua 1:8). However, it may be a smooth stone for them, but still a rough stone for us. Nevertheless, if we apply David's training regimen to our daily walk, we can be sure to sling smoothed-out stones as well.

Slinging Stones

"…And chose him five smooth stones out of the brook…" 1st Samuel 17:40

All that was written in this chapter thus far regarding meditation has led us to this point: to boldly take down giants. Knowing Jesus intimately in His Word will cause faith to rise to the occasion. Three main principles found within 1st Samuel 17:40 about David's implements coincide perfectly with our approach to battle today.

The first principle: Authority

"And he took his staff in his hand, and chose him five smooth stones out of the brook, and put them in a shepherd's bag which he had, even in a scrip; and his sling was in his hand: and he drew near to the Philistine." (1st Samuel 17:40)

David took his staff in his hand. We know that the staff represents authority. David went out to Goliath with the authority of God. Like Moses stood against Pharoah with the rod of God, so did David stand against Goliath with his shepherd's staff.

In Exodus 4, Moses threw his staff upon the ground, and it turned into a serpent. Then, in obedience to God's Word, Moses grabbed the serpent by the tail, signifying he had the power over it. This rod then became the tool used to pronounce judgment upon Pharaoh. Now, when you grab a snake by its head, it's because you're afraid of getting bit. However, when you grab it by the tail, despite the fact it can swing around and bite you, it proves you're not afraid. See, Jesus grabbed the serpent by the tail, and He used his staff, the cross, to do so.

We now have the authority to stand against the enemy in the finished works of Jesus through the cross of Calvary.

The second principle: Renewing the mind.

> *"...and chose him five smooth stones out of the brook, and put them in a shepherd's bag which he had, even in a scrip..." (1st Samuel 17:40)*

David then grabbed five smooth stones out of the brook and placed them in his shepherd's bag.

> *"And a river went out of Eden to water the garden; and from thence it was parted, and became into four heads." (Genesis 2:10)*

Most assuredly, we have a flowing brook in our shepherd's bag as well. In the depths of our spirit, where God Himself dwells, we have the river of Life! This river proceeds from God's throne (Revelation 22:1). Like Eden had a river that parted into four heads and watered the rest of the garden, so do we have a river of Life within that waters our whole being.

> *"He that believeth on me, as the scripture hath said, **out of his belly** shall flow rivers of living water." (John 7:38)*

> *"But whosoever drinketh of the water that I shall give him shall never thirst; but the water that I shall give him shall be **in him** a well of water*

***springing up** into everlasting life." (John 4:14) (emphasis mine)*

Out of *our belly* flows this river! It is a well, *within us*, springing up into everlasting life! There is a channel this river desires to flow through, to water the rest of our garden… and this channel is our soul. There are stones of truth within our soul that need to be smoothed out by the river of Life within our spirit. Not that the truth is not *already* truth, (as if to say the truth itself needs to be honed) but that it must be the absolute truth within our own minds. We must be totally persuaded. In fact, the roughness is within our own soul!

This smoothing process comes from saturating ourselves in God's Word, praying in the Holy Spirit, fasting, and spending intimate time in the presence of God. This will inevitably cause the dams and strongholds of unbelief to break within our soul. The river of Life will then flow through our soul and "smooth out" the rough areas of our mind. In turn, we will have a belly full of faith filled words to reach in and grab at any moment.

This is a powerful understanding. See, we have all that we will ever need already within us! It is a matter of releasing what we already have! Apart from the gifts of the Holy Spirit in operation, it is only through the renewing of our minds, by the washing of God's Word, that releases the river of Life within. Otherwise, doubt, fear, and unbelief remain as dams holding back the power of God.

I have heard it said that we must allow our head knowledge to become heart knowledge. In other words, we must allow what's in our head, to make its way to our heart. I disagree. I believe it is what's within our heart that must make its way to our head. This is "revelation" of scripture: when our mind catches up to what our born-again spirit already knows.

Smith Wigglesworth once wrote about a power outage in a particular city. I find it so pertinent, and so powerful, that it deserves to be quoted as it was written:

"I know that salvation, while it is a perfect work, is an insulation that may have any number of volts behind it. In the days when bare wires were laid,

when electric power was obtained from Niagara, I am told that there was a city whose lights suddenly went out. Following the wires, the repairmen came to a place where a cat had gotten on the wires, and the lights had been stopped. I find that the dynamo of heaven can be stopped with a smaller thing than a cat. An impure thought stops the circulation. An act can stop the growth of a believer." (Smith Wigglesworth Devotional)

Though the examples are different, the principle is not. The power of God is within us and needs an unobstructed channel in which to flow through.

In Smith's example, Niagara Falls was the source of power. This waterfall generated the electricity that flowed through the wires, that went into the city. Amazingly, about 600,000 gallons of water fall from Niagara every second. In the time it takes to read this sentence, nearly two million gallons of water just flowed over Niagara's edge. Needless to say, there is no lack of power on Niagara's end! Yet a small cat happened to obstruct the electricity generated for the whole city.

Unbelief can easily obstruct the power of God in our lives. We must therefore meditate upon the Word of God and allow the river of Life to wash away the doubt in our hearts. This is the smoothing process: removing the doubt from our soul!

> *"For verily I say unto you, That whosoever shall* ***say*** *unto this mountain, Be thou removed, and be thou cast into the sea; and shall* ***not doubt in his heart,*** *but shall believe that those things which he* ***saith*** *shall come to pass; he shall have whatsoever he* ***saith****." (Mark 11:23) (emphasis mine)*

Like the cat on the wires stopped the lights in the city, so will doubt in a believer's heart stop a mountain from being moved. On the other hand, one word spoken in pure faith will destroy a giant.

The third principle: Speaking in faith

> *"...and his sling was in his hand: and he drew near to the Philistine." (1st Samuel 17:40)*

Now that we have these smoothed out stones of truth within the riverbeds of our bellies, we too, *by faith*, can reach into them like David did into his shepherd's bag and place them upon the slings of our tongues. Then, *by faith*, we can confidently drive them right into the forehead of the contradicting circumstance. *Faith* will hit its mark every time!

Predominate Hand

> *"Among all this people there were seven hundred chosen men lefthanded... (Judges 20:16)*

The third principle David enacted in taking down Goliath coincides with an extraordinary account found within the book of Judges. Though there is much to be expounded upon concerning the account itself, there is a verse that pertains greatly to our exposition thus far. Without coincidence, "hitting the mark" is found in an Old Testament example concerning slinging stones. The Benjamites of Gibeah were the epitome of perfect marksmanship.

> *"...seven hundred chosen men* ***lefthanded****; every one could sling stones at an hair breadth, and* ***not miss****." (Judges 20:16)*

This is truly phenomenal. These men could sling stones at targets the thickness of a human hair and not miss! With that said, the word *miss* here is *hata*, which is one of the Hebrew words for *sin*. *Hata*: *to miss, to sin, to miss the goal or path of right and duty.*

Notice also how the scripture mentions them all being lefthanded. This, of course, is not without significance. Tying our discussion together regarding our minds being renewed through meditation, and the lefthanded children of Benjamin, reveals an undeniable kingdom reality.

> *"And he that* ***doubteth*** *is damned if he eat, because he eateth not of faith:* ***for whatsoever is not of faith is sin****." (Romans 14:23) (emphasis mine)*

According to this passage in Romans, whatever is not done in faith is sin. Therefore, words slang from our tongues with doubt will miss the mark. However, if we are like the lefthanded Benjamites, we'll never miss!

The name Benjamin joins two Hebrew words together. *Ben* means "*son*," and *Jamin* means "*right hand.*" Benjamin: "*Son of the right hand.*" Isn't it interesting how the name Benjamin means righthanded son… and these particular Benjamites were all lefthanded? They were seemingly going against their own name and nature! Truth be told, we are all sons and daughters of a natural predominance and must go against our old nature.

> *"Because the carnal mind is enmity against God...So then they that are in the flesh cannot please God." (Romans 8:7-8)*

The carnal, or predominantly natural way of thinking (according to the physical senses and ways of the flesh) is God's enemy. This, in fact, is more of an enemy to us than the devil. The devil knows this; therefore, he comes after the seeds of God's Word with all that he has so that we don't live according to faith: the friend of God! Abraham was the friend of God according to his faith! Now that we are in the faith, we must also renew our mind by an "unnatural" way of thinking. The things of the kingdom are at first unnatural to our unrenewed mind.

In speculation, I can hear the other tribe members of Benjamin saying, *"You know, we're all righties here! Our fathers are all righthanded; their father's... all righthanded; so, how is it that you're doing everything lefty?"* This would be the natural response from those walking according to the only way they are accustomed to. Nevertheless, despite all opposition, we must learn to walk according to the way we are *not* accustomed to.

"This is so unnatural!"

This is a common saying when trying to do something with our opposite hand, is it not?

In the beginning of my walk with God, I happened to be training for an upcoming "bare-knuckle" karate tournament. This only meant that we would compete without any gloves on. During our practice sparring session, my finger broke upon striking my opponent's elbow. I "missed the target" of his abdomen and paid the price! Unbeknownst to me, this would become quite the ordeal.

The way my finger broke was explained like this: imagine someone clean cutting a pencil in half and trying to put it back together (which was my case) versus snapping a pencil in half and trying to put it back together. Due to the pencil splintering, you're able to put it back together due to a snap. You could almost write with it again! Unfortunately, my finger couldn't be easily put back together because it was a clean break. So… I underwent surgery, had three temporary pins put in place to hold my pinky together, and then had a cast placed from my hand all the way up to my elbow to prevent my hand or finger from moving. My right arm was rendered useless!

For three months, I had to learn how to do everything lefthanded. As you could imagine, nearly everything felt unnatural. However, I did become quite the proficient lefthanded bowler, if I may say.

What the Lord revealed to me through this occurrence later in my walk with Him is how we must simply learn how to do things the way of the Spirit, which we are not accustomed to, instead of the ways of the flesh. It may feel unnatural at first, but before you know it, you'll be hitting a strike with your opposite hand every time. You'll be without unbelief, and you'll never *hata*. You won't ever miss the mark.

> *"But without faith it is impossible to please him: for he that cometh to God must believe that he is, and that he is a rewarder of them that diligently seek him." (Hebrews 11:6)*

8

Perfect Love

"Behold, what manner of love the Father hath bestowed upon us, that we should be called the sons of God..." (1st John 3:1)

Behold! What manner of love! What exactly was this love bestowed upon us by the Father? The love He gave us was His One and only Son. The manner of His love was the lengths He traveled to redeem us. The inevitability of the cross didn't stop Him from creating us, nor did He change His mind when the time came to carry it. He chose to innocently die with us in mind. In turn, we became the children of God. This is Perfect Love! The honor of kings is to cast our crowns at His feet and to rejoice in being called His sons and daughters.

This book has endeavored to prove how the matter worth searching was Jesus, but the clues along the way have been the clear expressions of His love. Truth be told, God's nature and character have been under attack since the Garden of Eden. Like the enemy did towards Eve, in making her question God's intentions towards her, he tries to do the same with us. He flips the script and portrays God as our enemy! He subtly accomplishes this through lies and fear. All the while, God has never failed us yet.

The Honor of Kings has essentially taken on the task of flipping the script back on the devil. Behind every tragedy, disappointment, and contradiction has been the thief. Contrarily, throughout this book, God's goodness and love have been revealed through otherwise hidden narratives. The devil didn't hide them… God did! This was not for his glory… but God's! The gold is greatest under the ground, and treasure worth holding is treasure worth searching for.

The devil tries, however, to take the scriptures out of context like he did while tempting Jesus. Fortunately, Jesus was quite familiar with the word.

He didn't entertain nor fall for his deception.

This is the whole point, my friends…neither should we!

> *"Then said Jesus to those Jews which believed on him, If ye* ***continue in my word****, then are ye my disciples indeed; And ye shall know the truth, and the truth shall make you free." (John 8:31-32) (emphasis mine)*

> *"As the Father hath loved me, so have I loved you:* ***continue ye in my love.****" (John 15:9) (emphasis mine)*

To know the truth and to be set free is to continue in His Word and to abide in His love. Adhering to Jesus' words will make us impervious to deception. The revelation is this: abiding in God's love is the ultimate honor of kings.

This final chapter will focus on the trunk of love and its branches of wisdom. Love is not something we learn in Christian elementary school and then move on from, but love is where we are to ever abide. Love is first, all encompassing, and never failing. Love is not only the ground in which we are rooted or the foundation in which we stand, but it is the fruit-bearing tree and the entire house.

If love is a filled house for the glory of God, then where does fear have a place? To the degree that we are filled with God's love is to the degree that fear is cast out. Perfect love (or rather matured and completed love in us) casts out fear (1st John 4:18). Though Solomon was the wisest to have ever lived, *besides Jesus, of course,* he failed to learn an important lesson from his father, David. Though wisdom was bountifully imparted for Solomon, evidently, love was not perfected.

Saul will also be mentioned in comparison to David's approach to leadership and why it is vital to fear God and not man. Sadly, Saul could have avoided all his trouble if he had only feared God.

When understanding and operating in perfected love, we will see how fear, in turn, will be eradicated. All kings mentioned in this book have either excelled or failed in understanding God's love and have either feared God or man as a result.

Lastly, wisdom will be our great reward for fearing the Lord. The fear of the Lord is wisdom's beginning. The Bible says that wisdom is supreme and mentions how it pleads with us to acquire understanding at all costs. Therefore, we will close out this chapter and book with the most valuable treasure of kings.

With that said, let's begin by introducing a man who had the greatest grasp on God's love. John seemed to have figured it out.

The One Whom Jesus Loves

Some may think that John was loved more than the other disciples because he literally introduced himself as "*The disciple whom Jesus loved*" (John 21:7). However, I disagree. It wasn't that God loved John more than the rest... it was that John *knew* God's love more than the rest. He *identified* himself as the one Jesus loved. It became his outlook on life. What a perspective! That's why there were the twelve, the three, and the one. John was the one. Would to God that we would grasp this revelation! *We* are the ones whom Jesus loves!

Isn't it interesting that we tell a new believer to start in the gospel of John rather than in Matthew, which starts the New Testament? This is because the gospel of John embodies God's love and supersedes the others without question. In fact, the gospel of John mentions love 22 times more than the other three gospels combined! The reason we tell a new disciple to start in the book of John is without coincidence. Love is preeminent.

John puts it best:

> *"We love him, because he first loved us." (1st John 4:19)*

Mankind was clueless as to what love was before Christ. Unfortunately, countless men and women are clueless still. Would you be frustrated with a blind man who couldn't travel without assistance? Shouldn't we expect they would need help? In the same way, the world is wrapped up in a self-seeking "love," and they assuredly need assistance. Consider Christ on the cross:

> *"Then said Jesus, Father, forgive them; for they know not what they do..." (Luke 23:34)*

Thank God for forgiving us because we didn't know what we were doing!

We were selfish and blind and in hopeless need of assistance! For us now in Christ, we *only* love because He first loved us. You know the popular phrase, "*Let me show you how it's done!*" Glory to God, we needed an example… and what a Perfect One given! Jesus did for us what the law couldn't: He showed us *how* to love our neighbor by loving us. We never deserved it! If we are waiting for some type of reciprocation from our spouse, family member, friend, co-worker, or even a stranger to love them, then we don't know what love is at all. If Jesus had thought this way, He would have never come.

> *"But God commendeth his love toward us, in that,* ***while we were yet sinners****, Christ died for us." (Romans 5:8) (emphasis mine)*

> *Concerning the law, Paul says in Romans that if we love one another, we have fulfilled it.*

> *"Owe no man any thing, but to love one another:* ***for he that loveth another hath fulfilled the law****." (Romans 13:8)*

What a relief! The law fulfilled through love! Now we have the capability to love our neighbor. Importantly, we were outcasts and Gentiles by nature and were never under the law to begin with. Thanks be to God that we weren't engrafted into the Old Testament law but rather into a New Covenant of love. The law fulfilled. Better yet, the finished works of Christ! Paul continues:

> *"For this, Thou shalt not commit adultery, Thou shalt not kill, Thou shalt not steal, Thou shalt not bear false witness, Thou shalt not covet; and if there be any other commandment, it is briefly comprehended in this saying, namely,* ***Thou shalt love thy neighbour as thyself. Love worketh no ill to his neighbour: therefore love is the fulfilling of the law****." (Romans 13:9-10)*

See, because I love my brother, I won't covet his possessions or desire his wife. Because I love my sister, I will not speak slanderously nor bear false witness against her. Because I love my neighbor, I will not steal from him. This is the good news! I don't have to fulfill the law; I just have to understand love fulfilled. The missing key was *always* love!

Paul explains love perfectly here in Corinthians:

> *"Love suffers long and is kind; love does not envy; love does not parade itself, is not puffed up; does not behave rudely, does not seek its own, is not provoked, thinks no evil; does not rejoice in iniquity, but rejoices in the truth; bears all things, believes all things, hopes all things, endures all things. Love never fails..." (1st Corinthians 13:4-8 NKJV)*

I'm sure you have heard a fellow believer at some point, jokingly or seriously, say, "*Don't pray for patience, God will give you situations that require it!*" All kidding aside, this couldn't be further from God's will. If God *is* love (1st John 4:8), and long suffering (patience) is mentioned as the first attribute of love here in Corinthians, then how could we ever say such a thing? Who are we aspiring to be like… Jesus, right?

Love doesn't envy, it is not selfish; love is not proud, nor does it boast. Love never fails.

Another attribute of God's love is that it rejoices in the truth. This is vital. One way to look at this is how we must rejoice in what God's Word says about us! If I were to guess why most Christians struggle with love, I would imagine it has something to do with rejoicing in the truth. Meaning, most Christians read a promise in the Bible and know it's true but subtly doubt instead of confidently rejoice. When we come across a passage that confronts the way we view ourselves, we must choose to rejoice in the truth over how our soul "feels" about it. The truth of how God sees us is not contingent on how we feel but rather on how He feels about us. He's never changing His mind. He loves you!

With that said, how can I love my neighbor as myself… if I don't love *myself*? This is why we *must* rejoice in the truth of what God's Word says about us. Now, this cannot be mistaken with loving the life Jesus said to lose for His sake… but loving the life He told us we'd find.

Can we learn from John's example?

If *we* are the ones whom Jesus loves, and God *so* loved the world… then we must receive His love with outstretched arms so we can love the world in turn. It is only pride to withstand God's love due to *whatever* reason we hold on to. To somehow believe that we are unworthy of God's love is equivalent to esteeming God as a liar. How? Well, because *He said* He loves you! We must humbly learn to accept His love because we can only give what we already have. We can only show forth the love of God to others as we have already received for ourselves. Therefore, love is not a big deal… it's pretty much the only deal.

I have often heard from others, *"I'm just not sure if God really loves me. I mean, I know the Bible says He loves me, but… I'm just not really sure."* Truth be told, what they are actually saying is they don't always *feel* like He loves them. Let this sink down deep: we can never, ever go based on how we feel when it comes to God's love for us. His love for us is steadfast. It is more faithful than the rising sun.

Though the sky might be overcast, and perpetual rain may consume the day, one would never question *if* the sun were in the sky. The weather may change from moment to moment, but the Bible says that as long as the earth remains, day and night will never cease (Genesis 8:22). Though days could seem like nights on this side of heaven, the sun is high in the sky regardless. It is still day at 11 am, regardless of what it looks or feels like! If our emotions are like the weather, we will be doubleminded like James says and be as a wave in the sea is tossed. Knowing this, we must anchor our soul in the Rock, which is Christ, and never in the weather.

Looking unto our circumstances or emotions to determine if God loves us is like questioning if the sun ever rose because all we see are rainclouds. *"Does God love me today? I'm just not sure…."* Rest assured, we never have to be discouraged, nor do we ever have to wonder if God loves us. Moreover, this is how we can always know how much He does. This is the only way to know for sure:

> *"In this was manifested the love of God toward us, because that God sent his only begotten Son into the world, that we might live through him. Herein is love, not that we loved God, but that he loved us, and sent his Son to be the propitiation for our sins." (1st John 4:9-10)*

…The WORD!

Jesus demonstrated and manifested His love towards us when He died on the cross in our place. I'm sure He didn't *feel* like going to the cross. Love compelled Him to despise the shame and to consider the joy set before Him (Hebrews 12:2). His joy was inheriting us! He put a stake in the ground on Calvary's hill and died on it. This forever settled if God loved us or not.

In light of this, don't you ever let the devil deceive you again into thinking you're unworthy of His love. There is no condemnation for those who are in Christ. Jesus didn't become condemned so we could be condemned. We already were! He became condemned so we could be set free.

If you have Christ and you have truly repented; if you've long since confessed whatever you fell short in before the Lord… you have been cleansed from that sin and were washed from all unrighteousness. For Jesus' sake, you must now choose to believe it! Once, you *were* unworthy, but now you *are* forever His. You are loved, you are forgiven, and you are not condemned.

> ***"For God so loved the world, that he gave his only begotten Son,*** *that whosoever believeth in him should not perish, but have everlasting life. For God sent not his Son into the world to condemn the world; but that the world through him might be saved." (John 3:16-17) (emphasis mine)*

Fear in The Night

> *"...perfect love casteth out fear: because fear hath torment..." (1st John 4:18)*

The Lord consistently declares throughout the Bible to *"Fear not"* and *"Do not be afraid!"* The best Biblical approach to not being afraid is not to face our fears but to get in love. To abide in God's love is to cast out fear by default because perfect love casts out fear.

Solomon should have had the greatest grasp on conquering fear because he had the greatest grasp on knowledge and wisdom, but he didn't. Unfortunately, Solomon writes in his song that he feared in the night as he lied in his bed. Who could know for certain how long this fearful season was for him? But what he says regarding it should spare us from his experience.

> *"Behold his bed, which is Solomon's; threescore valiant men are about it, of the valiant of Israel. They all hold swords, being expert in war: every man hath his sword upon his thigh because of fear in the night." (Song of Solomon 3:7-8)*

I will preface what's said next by granting the possibility that this passage is allegorical and not really the case for Solomon. Nevertheless, the first rule of prophecy is to take everything literally unless it is proven that you can't. *"Pluck out your eye,"* or *"Cut off your right hand,"* for instance. With that said, I am relatively safe because I'm expounding upon it as a typology anyway. Although, I will first touch on aspects of this passage as if it were the case for Solomon because His father, David, provides a necessary contrast.

There are a few things worth mentioning here, but the first would be to address the elephant in the room, and that is... *what an enormous bed!* Two elephants would fit in this one! King Solomon had 60 expert warriors armed for battle facing north, south, east, and west. I picture 15 men about-facing Solomon on all four sides of his king-sized bed.

Along these lines, consider the particular reason they are positioned there in the first place:

> *"...every man hath his sword upon his thigh* ***because of fear in the night****." (Song of Solomon 3:8)*

What's interesting is how what's specifically mentioned is not for an ambush, or for battle, or to protect the king... but for fear in the night! Consider what the Lord Himself said Solomon's reign would consist of:

> *"Behold, a son shall be born to thee, who shall be a man of rest; and I will give him rest from all his enemies round about: for his name shall be Solomon, and I will give peace and quietness unto Israel in his days." (1st Chronicles 22:9)*

Solomon was established according to his own name. Solomon was granted supernatural peace and rest. We have learned how Solomon represents us as the church and how Christ reigns as the Prince of Peace through us today. If we are the New Testament "Solomon's", then it is imperative to know what our names and positions truly consist of.

Now, I could understand if David, being a man of war, had his armed men surrounding his bed at all times. However, I can never understand it to be the case for Solomon. Wasn't he given rest from God on all sides from his enemies?

Consider his father, David, and a few of the psalms he wrote:

> *"I will both lay me down in peace, and sleep: for thou, LORD, only makest me dwell in safety." (Psalm 4:8)*

> *"Lord, how are they increased that trouble me! many are they that rise up against me…I cried unto the LORD with my voice, and he heard me out of his holy hill. Selah. I laid me down and slept; I awaked; for the LORD sustained me. I will not be afraid of ten thousands of people, that have set themselves against me round about." (Psalm 3:1, 4-6)*

David slept in peace in the midst of many enemies! Some were Saul, the relentless Philistines, and even his son Absalom. If anyone had the right to bunker down in his bed, it was him! This is a perfect scripture to summarize the difference between fearing man and fearing the Lord. Because David feared the Lord, he was able to sleep peacefully despite being in perpetual war. Whereas Solomon had a reign of peace, yet he slept in fear.

David often found himself in daunting situations with many enemies seeking his life. Like David, Jesus had many enemies as well. Sadly, it wound up being His own people. They weren't the Philistines but the Pharisees. Despite many demonically influenced religious leaders seeking to destroy Jesus, He was never afraid. He was able to lie down in peace wherever he was. Whether that be in a wilderness with wild animals and the devil or in a boat in the midst of a tempestuous sea: Jesus slept in perfect peace!

Moreover… how could love fear? That would be the ultimate contradiction. Being that He never feared because He was love… He is our ultimate example! Now, if God is love…*and as He is, so are we in this world*…do we ever have reason to fear? No! We only have the opportunity for His love to be shown through us! We are called to shine in dark places, not to blend in.

Why is a child afraid of the dark until their parents turn the light on? Once the light is switched on, they immediately find comfort. With us, we have had the light turned on for good. The light of the world is not only shining upon us but within us. How can we fear if we are the children of light (John 12:36, Ephesians 5:8, 1st Thessalonians 5:5)?

"...He that feareth is not made perfect in love." (1st John 4:18)

Though the love of God has been shed abroad in our hearts (Romans 5:5), the *only* reason we fear is that we have not allowed His love to be poured into our souls. Though we have absolute light in our spirit, our soul could be like a darkened curtain. We cannot afford to poke a few holes in it; we must remove it altogether! Moreover, to neglect the work of God's love within our souls is to permit the hold fear has by default.

Touching back on Solomon's Song:

...They all hold swords, being expert in war... (Song of Solomon 3:8)

Have you ever considered these "expert warriors" King Solomon had stationed at his bedside? Have you ever wondered, *"Where did they learn war?"* If Solomon was established in rest, when did they become experts in war? More specifically, *where* did they learn war? See, the men of war guarding the king for fear in the night hadn't fought a battle since they served under King David. Solomon inherited his father David's warriors!

Imagine with me for a moment what these men could have been thinking as they, night after night, encamped around the king. Perhaps they thought it was a bit ridiculous? Maybe unseemly for a king of peace? Especially how he wasn't at war. His father, David, had fought all the battles!

Perhaps it is not a great stretch to imagine how these warriors could represent angels today. Perhaps the angels are confused as to why we are afraid of what Jesus has already subdued. Jesus won the war for us. He defeated the enemy! Our Father established us in righteousness, peace, and joy in the Holy Spirit. There is nothing left to fear. However, some of us find ourselves afraid of the shadows when Jesus destroyed the substance.

Like Solomon was in paranoia and fear in the night over the shadows, so do many Christians fear the devil when he has been completely stripped of all his authority and power over us (Matthew 28:18-19, Luke 10:19,

Colossians 2:15. Hebrews 2:14). The only power he has is the power we give over through fear. Therefore, the best way to resist his attacks is to saturate ourselves in God's love because:

> *"...perfect love casteth out fear... (1st John 4:18)*

Now, there is a world of difference between being fearful, and fearing God. One is filled with life, and the other, death.

> *"The fear of the LORD is clean, enduring for ever: the judgments of the LORD are true and righteous altogether." (Psalm 19:9)*

Fearing God was something David knew firsthand. Saul, on the other hand, feared all but God. Saul's leadership approach was that of selfishness. This is a contradiction to God's love. David and Saul provide excellent leadership examples for us to glean from. Only one, however, feared properly.

The Beginning of Wisdom

> *"The fear of the LORD is the beginning of wisdom: and the knowledge of the holy is understanding." (Proverbs 9:10)*

The fear of the Lord is the key to opening wisdom's door. The Bible says that wisdom is the principal thing in life:

> *"Wisdom is the principal thing; therefore get wisdom: and with all thy getting get understanding." (Proverbs 4:7)*

The opening verse states how the fear of the Lord is the beginning of wisdom, and the following verse shows us how wisdom is of highest importance. So, if fearing God grants us the principal matter, why are we foolishly fearing all else?

> *"And Saul said unto Samuel, I have sinned: for I have transgressed the commandment of the LORD, and thy words:* ***because I feared the people, and obeyed their voice.****" (1st Samuel 15:24) (emphasis mine)*

Saul, after dishonoring God, wanted to be honored before his people. How backwards! Notice also how this passage below ends:

> *"Then he said, I have sinned:* ***yet honour me now, I pray thee, before the elders of my people, and before Israel****, and turn again with me, that I may worship the LORD* ***thy*** *God." (1st Samuel 15:30)*

He was only considering himself. Saul's failures provide great admonitions for us in regard to leadership. Though we are called to serve and put others first, it is never at the expense of putting the Lord first. We should never consider the "voice of the people" if it's not the voice of God. There is a natural fear of man that needs to be put to death in order to live for the Lord. Otherwise, we will sell cheaply and compromise in critical situations. If the fear of the Lord is the beginning of wisdom, then the fear of man is the beginning of foolishness.

Saul seemed to struggle greatly with what others thought about him. This can never be a trait of any successful leader in God's kingdom. Saul's consideration of others was quite literally his downfall. If he hadn't listened to the counsel of his people, but obeyed God instead, he would have had his kingdom established forever according to scripture.

Some may say, *"Well, you know... you just have to use wisdom!"* This is a snare and a faith killer!

> *"The fear of man bringeth a snare: but whoso putteth his trust in the LORD shall be safe." (Proverbs 29:25)*

If the fear of man brings a trap... then the fear of the Lord brings freedom!

My response to the *"You just have to use wisdom"* statement has always been, *"Well, who's wisdom?"* The wisdom of man will almost always contradict the wisdom of God. They are diametrically opposed. Truthfully, any wisdom of man that doesn't contradict God came from above anyway! Earthly wisdom is sensual and demonic (James 3:15). When talking about stepping out for God, countless Christians have been paralyzed by worldly wisdom.

> *"Samuel also said unto Saul, The LORD sent me to anoint thee to be king over his people Israel: now therefore hearken thou unto the voice of the* ***words of the LORD****...Now go and smite Amalek, and* ***utterly destroy all that they have, and spare them not;*** *but slay both man and*

woman, infant and suckling, ox and sheep, camel and ass." (1st Samuel 15:1, 3) (emphasis mine)

It might have seemed foolish to Saul's men to kill all the animals in the Amalekite city, but what was more foolish was for Saul to have listened to them. He received a direct word from the Lord through the prophet Samuel! However, Saul completely disregarded God's ways in order to oblige the ways of his men.

With that said, let's briefly sidetrack and then continue where we left off with Saul.

Kingdom Wisdom/Worldly Wisdom

In regard to Saul receiving a direct word from the Lord, we have also received a direct word from God as well. It's called the Bible! Oftentimes, we reason ourselves out of performing what the Lord has called us to do. He has told us to heal the sick, but some of us wonder, *"What if I get sick myself?"* Again, this type of wisdom is natural and sense based. It negates faith by its logical approach. Nature has taught us to stay away from those who have contagious diseases… but we have a new nature. The Word of God goes directly against this world's "wisdom." "This wisdom descendeth not from above, but is earthly, sensual, devilish." (James 3:15)

The wisdom of this world was never generated from God but from sin and the devil. This carnal wisdom is paralyzing to our faith. This thinking ultimately stems from fear. Unfortunately, we have been shaped and molded by this way of thinking before receiving Jesus.

With that said, why would Jesus tell us to cleanse the leper if we would become leprous? Why would he tell us to heal the sick… if we would straightway need someone to then pray for us? What a contradiction! Leprosy is a contagious disease, yet Jesus confronted it hands on. He didn't seem to use "wisdom."

When dealing with a backache, or foot pain, some of us would be confident to lay hands and pray. Yet when dealing with the flu and different kinds of viruses, we may think, *"Well... we should use wisdom here! We should pray from a distance. You know, God is not limited by distance. Remember? He spoke a word, and the Centurion's servant was healed!"* Can

I be bold and call this out for what it is? It is nothing but fear.

You may think, *"David! Didn't God give us a brain?"* I would say, *"Yes, and often times it's what hinders His work here through it."*

See, Jesus *touched* the leper. He didn't merely "touch" him through prayer… He *physically* touched Him and healed him. How was Jesus able to do this? He knew His authority, He knew the law of sin and death, and ultimately, He operated through love and not fear.

Now, am I saying that we should run to the nearest leper colony and heal them? Well… yes and no. We are called to do so… however, it is not presumption that blesses God, but faith. Presumption is without substance; faith *is* substance (Hebrews 11:1).

The point is… if we know we are called to do the works that Jesus did (and, in fact, greater works), then what is stopping us but fear? Fear of the unknown, fear of failing, fear of getting sick, fear of… *its all fear!* The good news is that we don't have to acquire many loves to conquer our many fears. We just need His all-encompassing Love to eradicate them all. Abiding in God's love is what grants us the ability to walk in His authority and power. Then, we are unafraid of what this world and its ways can do, but we fear God and keep His commandments instead (1st John 3:22-24). His commandments are not grievous nor impossible to perform (1st John 5:3). His commandment is love (2nd John 1:6). By this, faith operates (Galatians 5:6).

By walking in love, we are operating according to the ways of the kingdom. The kingdom of God supersedes the laws of the earth. The kingdom of God is the system of higher rank.

Unfortunately, we have mingled worldly logic and heavenly wisdom when walking out our salvation with fear and trembling. We have fearfully trembled at the kingdom of darkness instead of fearing God and boldly standing against it. We have all been, *and in many ways are still*, guilty of this. This is like mixing clay and steel! Nevertheless, the wisdom that comes from above is unmingled and undiluted:

> *"But the wisdom that is from above is first pure, then peaceable, gentle, and easy to be intreated, full of mercy and good fruits, without*

partiality, and without hypocrisy." (James 3:17)

Now, let's get back to presumption…

First, in order to operate in unobstructed faith, we must eventually submit to this reality: doubt and hesitation will inoculate us. My friends… doubt is the issue at hand! We have the faith necessary if we only remove the doubt! If doubt is not removed, we will go forth in presumption, not faith. Instead of being immune to the sickness in which we are told to drive away, we could open the door to fear and become susceptible. We would then fall due to an ignorance of our rights as kingdom citizens.

Look at it like this. If I am told in scripture that all animals are subject unto me, but a roaring lion were to appear out of nowhere and seek to overtake me… fight or flight would be engaged. Though the scripture *says* I have authority over the animal kingdom, it is only if I wholeheartedly believe this *before* I'm confronted with a lion. If I don't meditate on the surety of God's Word to overcome my sensual wisdom and logic first, only flight will kick in when faced with fear. To have fight engaged during the confrontation is to have the fight of faith engaged beforehand. The good fight of faith is one in which we ever stand in God's armament. Truly, we have authority over the animal kingdom… so long as we believe it!

Now, I would not advise on aggravating lions or foolishly taking up snakes. Though we have authority, this is a misunderstanding of scripture at best. Those who do such things would be defining presumption altogether. That said, the gospel consists of taking back our ground for the kingdom of God by confronting the works of darkness head on. Some of that ground is occupied by lion-like adversaries. Whether they be demonic forces, death, plagues, or diseases, their illegal holds upon the hearts of men are only conquered by love.

This whole book could be summed up in this one phrase: *to abide in God's love and to walk in the freedom Jesus paid the price for is to make way for others to follow suit.* This cannot be emphasized enough! It is of the utmost importance to abide in His love. Nothing else in regard to wisdom applies if not overwhelmed in the love of God. If not for the love of God, we will presume we can raise the dead, heal the sick, cast out devils… but we will never be in pure faith. We will find ourselves rooted partly in the kingdom's wisdom and partly in the world's. The moment a storm comes, our tree will crack in half.

With that said… let's get back on track with Saul!

Fear Of Man

"And he took Agag the king of the Amalekites alive, and utterly destroyed all the people with the edge of the sword. ***But Saul and the people spared Agag, and the best of the sheep****, and of the oxen, and of the fatlings, and the lambs, and all that was good, and would not utterly destroy them: but every thing that was vile and refuse, that they destroyed utterly." (1st Samuel 15:8-9) (emphasis mine)*

Look at the unfortunate chain of events that followed Saul's disobedience. The worst part is how this could've all been avoided if he only feared God.

"And Samuel came to Saul: and Saul said unto him, Blessed be thou of the LORD: I have performed the commandment of the LORD." (1st Samuel 15:13)

Wow, what boldness! Not for the good, however. Saul *knew* he didn't follow through completely with what the Lord commanded. He was just trying to cover himself. Though Saul was lying to the prophet Samuel, he was ultimately lying to God. Needless to say, Saul stood no chance whatsoever.

"And Samuel said, What meaneth then this bleating of the sheep in mine ears, and the lowing of the oxen which I hear? And Saul said, They have brought them from the Amalekites: ***for the people spared the best of the sheep and of the oxen****, to sacrifice unto the LORD thy God; and the rest we have utterly destroyed." (1st Samuel 15:14-15)*

Now Saul blamed it on the people! There was no one to blame but himself.

"Then Samuel said unto Saul, Stay, and I will tell thee what the LORD hath said to me this night. And he said unto him, Say on…the LORD sent thee on a journey, and said, Go and utterly destroy the sinners the Amalekites, and fight against them until they be consumed. ***Wherefore***

> ***then didst thou not obey the voice of the LORD,*** *but didst fly upon the spoil, and didst evil in the sight of the LORD? And Saul said unto Samuel,* ***Yea, I have obeyed the voice of the LORD, and have gone the way which the LORD sent me****, and have brought Agag the king of Amalek, and have utterly destroyed the Amalekites." (1st Samuel 15:16-20) (emphasis mine)*

Have you ever been embarrassed for someone else in a humiliating situation? I'm sure your face has turned red for someone acting foolishly in a classroom at some point, waiting for the teacher to reprimand them! What awkwardness and built-up pressure, right? This is how I feel each time I read this account. Samuel is about to punish Saul for his foolishness, and I cannot help but experience a bit of awkward pressure each time I read about it. Saul is openly lying to perhaps the most accurate prophet to have ever lived!

Saul then tries to lighten the impending blow from Samuel by saying that the people took of the spoil in order to sacrifice unto the Lord. Even if this were true, it was absolute disobedience regardless. Additionally, he is once again shifting blame and trying to cover his sin. This, of course, does not turn out well for him. Saul finally reveals the truth at the end of this account in that he feared the people. At this point, it was much too late. For me, Saul's "repentance" seemed disingenuous. I'm sure he was remorseful for having lost the kingdom, as Esau was for losing his birthright, but it seemed that Saul exhausted all of his options and eventually "gave in."

> *"But the people took of the spoil, sheep and oxen, the chief of the things which should have been utterly destroyed, to sacrifice unto the LORD thy God in Gilgal. And Samuel said, Hath the LORD as great delight in burnt offerings and sacrifices, as in obeying the voice of the LORD? Behold, to obey is better than sacrifice, and to hearken than the fat of rams. For rebellion is as the sin of witchcraft, and stubbornness is as iniquity and idolatry. Because thou hast rejected the word of the LORD, he hath also rejected thee from being king. And Saul said unto Samuel, I have sinned: for I have transgressed the commandment of the LORD, and thy words: because I feared the people, and obeyed their voice. (1st Samuel 15:21-24)*

Amongst many things said in this paragraph, this stands out to me:

"...to sacrifice unto the LORD thy God in Gilgal" (1st Samuel 15:21)

Isn't it interesting that Saul said *thy* God instead of saying *my* God, or even just *the* Lord God? Doesn't this seem impersonal to you? Or worse yet, could it imply a lack of relationship with the Lord altogether? He also says this in the 30th verse when asking to be honored before the elders and his people.

After this, Saul asks *Samuel* to pardon his sin. Wouldn't you cry out to *the Lord* for sinning? This is what David did.

"And David said unto Nathan, I have sinned against the LORD. And Nathan said unto David, The LORD also hath put away thy sin; thou shalt not die." (2nd Samuel 12:13)

"Against thee, thee only, have I sinned, and done this evil in thy sight: that thou mightest be justified when thou speakest, and be clear when thou judgest." (Psalm 51:4)

David's sin was pardoned by the prophet because he cried out unto God. For Saul, his repentance was more like being sorry for being caught but not truly sorry for what he failed to follow through with from the start! In the beginning of this chapter, the Lord revealed to Samuel that Saul turned back from following Him:

"Then came the word of the LORD unto Samuel, saying, It repenteth me that I have set up Saul to be king: ***for he is turned back from following me, and hath not performed my commandments.*** *And it grieved Samuel; and he cried unto the LORD all night." (1st Samuel 15:10-11) (emphasis mine)*

We also know that Saul was a repeat offender in regard to transgressing God's commandments. While in Gilgal, Saul feared and found himself under pressure. He failed to wait for Samuel and performed a sacrifice without right. When confronted, he accused the people of scattering and for Samuel not arriving on time! Essentially, Saul said he had no option but to perform a sacrifice without him. Saul again shifted the blame unto others. For us as leaders, pressure and obligation should *never* force us to act. We should always be led by peace, especially when under pressure. Below is the beginning of Saul's end. Be sure to notice who's God he mentions once more:

> *"And he tarried seven days, according to the set time that Samuel had appointed: but Samuel came not to Gilgal; and the people were scattered from him. And Saul said, Bring hither a burnt offering to me, and peace offerings. And he offered the burnt offering. And it came to pass, that as soon as he had made an end of offering the burnt offering, behold, Samuel came; and Saul went out to meet him, that he might salute him. And Samuel said, What hast thou done? And Saul said, Because I saw that the people were scattered from me, and that thou camest not within the days appointed, and that the Philistines gathered themselves together at Michmash; Therefore said I, The Philistines will come down now upon me to Gilgal, and I have not made supplication unto the LORD: I forced myself therefore, and offered a burnt offering. And Samuel said to Saul, Thou hast done foolishly: thou hast not kept the commandment of the LORD thy God, which he commanded thee: for now would the LORD have established thy kingdom upon Israel for ever. But now thy kingdom shall not continue: the LORD hath sought him a man after his own heart, and the LORD hath commanded him to be captain over his people, because thou hast not kept that which the LORD commanded thee." (1st Samuel 13:8-14)*

One of the most important things for us as leaders to do is to take accountability for our actions. This should go without saying, but we are accountable for our decisions, whether right or wrong. We must own up to our mistakes and be humble! Humility, transparency, repentance, and confession of faults when wrong are essential character traits and godly habits of any successful leader. When we are trying to find ways out of messes by blaming the contrary circumstances, or worse yet, our brothers and sisters, we are operating out of self-centeredness and pride. We got blame shifting from Adam, but we got agape love from the Last Adam.

Wise Counsel

> *"And David behaved himself wisely in all his ways; and the LORD was with him." (1st Samuel 18:14)*

David was wise because he feared God. Unlike Saul, who allowed his people to set the course for his kingdom's reign, David chose God's ways over the people's.

> *"Where no counsel is, the people fall: but in the multitude of counsellers there is safety." (Proverbs 11:14)*

Yes, there is safety in the multitude of counselors… so long as they are speaking according to God's Word and ways! Otherwise, it is just more unbelief in need of washing away with God's Word in the first place.

> *"There is a way which seemeth right unto a man, but the end thereof are the ways of death." (Proverbs 14:12)*

You can have a multitude of counselors speaking on behalf of the way that seems right! There's no safety in that at all. In fact, it's detrimental. A "good" counselor is one who never ceases to remind you of what God's Word says. On the other hand, you could have a multitude of counselors around you, leading you to death! If we are not aware, we will use caution, consideration, care, and concern as means to safeguard our walk with God… all under the guise of wisdom. It is not wisdom at all. It is fear. Again, the fear of man is a snare. The ways of the world are as fetters to the ankles in regard to walking with God.

As leaders, we cannot afford to lean onto our own understanding nor rely on the understanding of others if it doesn't coincide with scripture. Case closed! The way that seems right leads to death. There is only one way that leads to life: *to fear the Lord!*

> *"The fear of the LORD tendeth [leads] to life: and he that hath it shall abide satisfied; he shall not be visited with evil." (Proverbs 19:23) (brackets mine)*

The way of wisdom is to choose God's ways over all others. Despite the pressures or consequences, the only counsel we are to adhere to is the Lord's.

This is the summary of the matter… to obey God's Word is to fear the Lord.

David behaved wisely in all *his* ways because he continuously sought *God's* ways. He knew the Lord's ways were higher, so he relentlessly cried after God's instead of implementing his own. This is exactly what eating from the tree of life instead of the knowledge of good and evil is all about.

Tree Of Life

> *Happy is the man that findeth wisdom, and the man that getteth understanding. For the merchandise of it is better than the merchandise of silver, and the gain thereof than fine gold. She is more precious than rubies: and all the things thou canst desire are not to be compared unto her. Length of days is in her right hand; and in her left hand riches and honour. Her ways are ways of pleasantness, and all her paths are peace. She is a tree of life to them that lay hold upon her: and happy is every one that retaineth her. (Proverbs 3:13-18)*

The evil on the tree was not how the enemy convinced Eve to eat from it, but the good. The "desire to make one wise" was its appeal (Genesis 3:6). How foolish!

In the same way, we may eat from the wrong tree when making our decisions. Though we may be eating from the good on the tree, and not the evil, it still inevitably leads to death. We may consider, contemplate, and muse over the knowledge of the best decision and miss out on the Lord's desired plan altogether.

Remember, the Lord knows the plans He has for us (Jeremiah 29:11). Take a deep breath and relax. You don't have to know it, you just have to trust that He does!

Even so, the Lord is not opposed to asking us to say yes to decisions that defy logic. The fruit of the tree of life is often against our reason but never without peace. There were times when the "best" decision for me was not God's decision at all. The way that *seemed* right unto me could have led me far from God's intended path. Sometimes we are asked to do what appears to be the least likely of all options! Truthfully, the way we know which option is from God is never through reason but only peace.

"And let the peace of God rule in your hearts, to which also you were called in one body; and be thankful." (Colossians 3:15)

Now, there is an instance with David that pertains greatly to our discussion. He is under attack from the Philistines and seeks the Lord for permission to battle. This account is one of the greatest examples of how to form a battle strategy. It was not in the method of the tactics, but in the method of his approach. Moreover, it was not his approach to the battle, but unto God.

"The Philistines also came and spread themselves in the valley of Rephaim. And David enquired of the LORD, saying, Shall I go up to the Philistines? wilt thou deliver them into mine hand? And the LORD said unto David, Go up: for I will doubtless deliver the Philistines into thine hand. And David came to Baalperazim, and David smote them there, and said, The LORD hath broken forth upon mine enemies before me, as the breach of waters. Therefore he called the name of that place Baalperazim." (2nd Samuel 5:18-20)

The Philistines gathered in Rephaim's valley, and David enquired of the Lord. David *always* enquired of the Lord. This is what set him apart from all other kings. In fact, his descendants were measured by his standard. David desired to establish God's kingdom. Unlike most kings, he didn't seek to build his own.

Following along, we see a similar attack from the Philistines:

*"And the Philistines **came up yet again**, and spread themselves in the **valley of Rephaim. And when David enquired of the LORD**, he said, Thou shalt not go up; but fetch a compass behind them, and come upon them over against the mulberry trees. And let it be, when thou hearest the sound of a going in the tops of the mulberry trees, that then thou shalt bestir thyself: for then shall the LORD go out before thee, to smite the host of the Philistines. And David did so, as the LORD had commanded him; and smote the Philistines from Geba until thou come to Gazer." (2nd Samuel 5:22-25)*

What's notable about this account is how both times the Philistines, and

David, did the same thing. The Philistine's chose to gather themselves in the same valley and David chose to enquire of the Lord. However, the Lord's battle plan was different this time. David wasn't going to attack them in the same manner as the last time. He would wait for the sound of wind against the mulberry trees and ambush them from behind.

There is much to consider about this for us today! Notice how David did not rely on what had worked in the last attack just a short while before, but instead, he chose to seek the Lord. This was his battle strategy! Though he could have easily relied on the "good knowledge" of the tree of his reason and logic, he chose to eat from the tree of Life. Good thing because David would have been blindsided if he chose to attack in the way God instructed him last. Instead, he blindsided them. This wisdom comes from God alone.

> *"Trust in the LORD with all thine heart; and lean not unto thine own understanding. In all thy ways acknowledge him, and he shall direct thy paths." (Proverbs 3:5-6)*

Like David, we must always seek the Lord in what to do! The sooner we realize we are stewards and not owners, is the sooner we begin to experience the abundant grace of God.

> *"For in him we live, and move, and have our being..." (Acts 17:28)*

It gives Him great pleasure when His children set their affection on Him and not their own intentions. It is not about seeking the way in which to go, but about seeking Him, the Way! He is the journey and the destination. See, this is called *relationship*. We can never get too wrapped up on principles and miss the principal thing: wisdom!

> *"But of him are ye in Christ Jesus,* ***who of God is made unto us wisdom****, and righteousness, and sanctification, and redemption." (1st Corinthians 1:30)*

Jesus *is* our wisdom!

Therefore... if the fear of the Lord is the beginning of wisdom, then to fear God is to begin to know Jesus! This is why wisdom is the *principal* thing because *Jesus* has been made unto us wisdom! To fear the Lord is to seek God's ways, not our own. To put what seems right to us down and trust Him with all our hearts. It is to put Him first, regardless of what it looks like. This is wisdom's way.

In closing, it is only fitting to end with the greatest of Solomon's wisdom:

> *"Let us hear the conclusion of the whole matter: Fear God, and keep his commandments: for this is the whole duty of man." (Ecclesiastes 12:13)*

For more information contact:

David Ravella
C/O Advantage Books
info@advbooks.com

To purchase additional copies of these books, visit our bookstore at
www.advbookstore.com

Orlando, Florida, USA
"we bring dreams to life"™
www.advbookstore.com